BFI Modern Classics

W9-AVQ-797

Rob White
Series Editor

BFI Modern Classics is a series of critical studies of films produced over
the last three decades. Writers explore their chosen films, offering a
range of perspectives on the dominant art and entertainment medium in
contemporary culture. The series gathers together snapshots of our
passion for and understanding of recent movies.

Also Published

The Thin Red Line
Michel Chion

(see a full list of titles in the series
at the back of this book)

History, Neo said, is a nightmare from which I am trying to awake ...

The Matrix

Joshua Clover

 Publishing

First published in 2004 by the
British Film Institute
21 Stephen Street, London W1T 1LN

The British Film Institute promotes greater
understanding and appreciation of,
and access to, film and moving image
culture in the UK.

Series design by Andrew Barron
& Collis Clements Associates

Typeset in Italian Garamond
and Swiss 721BT by
D R Bungay Associates,
Burghfield, Berks

Printed in the UK by
Norwich Colour Print, Drayton, Norfolk

British Library Cataloguing-in-Publication Data
A catalogue record for this book is available
from the British Library

ISBN 1-84457-045-2

Contents

1 Edge of the Construct

NEO: **Is that – ?**
CYPHER: **The Matrix? Yeah.**
NEO: **Do you always look at it encoded?**
CYPHER: **Well you have to. The image translators work for the
construct program. But there's way too much information to decode
the Matrix. You get used to it. I don't even see the code, all I see is
blond, brunette, redhead ...**

This particular moment was decisively popular around the time of *The
Matrix* (1999). The main character has come to suspect, or realise, that
what he had thought was reality is in fact a simulation of incredible power
and subtlety – one meant to deceive him, and perhaps everyone, generally
toward strange and malevolent ends.

Neo (Keanu Reeves) has just walked in on Cypher (Joe Pantoliano)
seated in front of more than a dozen flat-screen panels, down several of
which flow never-ending streams of eerie green characters – the iconic
image used for the film's title sequence and advertising. This is the Matrix,
the world of appearances, in its true form: just a bunch of computer code.

Cypher, and perhaps this is how he acquired his name, has become
so adept at decoding on the fly, in *real time*, that he no longer sees the code

itself. Instead he sees right through it, as if looking not at screens but at windows, streaked only with green rain, into the total virtual world that gives the movie its name.

In *The Truman Show* (1998), the hero's home town and the surrounding area turn out to be the world's largest soundstage, and he the star of the most popular and longest-running television show in history. *Dark City* (1998), in many ways the night-time version of *The Truman Show*, conjures a decrepit urban labyrinth eventually revealed to have been built by aliens for observing human behaviour; they want to understand exactly what a soul is. In *The Thirteenth Floor* (1999), one of the scientists engaged in perfecting a sim-city realises slowly that he himself, and

'You get used to it. I don't even see the code ...'

everything he knows, exists merely as part of another sim. This film is actually a remake of the 1973 Werner Fassbinder telefilm *World on a Wire*, featuring a computer named Simulacron; that this particular story seemed apt for revisiting just then, when everyone was filming a version of the story, is a particularly telling fact.

When Neo interrupts Cypher's reverie of code, he already knows that he's been trapped in the Matrix. He's already taken the red pill offered by rebel leader Morpheus (Laurence Fishburne), been released from his long sleep, and had the truth – of the machines' victory and humanity's thralldom – explained to him. Standing there before the grungy panoply of displays isn't truly the moment of revelation. It is, rather, the moment in which the hero sees the simulation as nothing more (and nothing less) than what it is, recognises the limited apparatus of what he once thought was infinite reality.[1]

What the hero sees in this moment, we might call 'The Edge of the Construct'. Indeed, we could apply that name to the microgenre itself, insofar as each story revolves around variations of this scene. Truman Burbank, having guessed at the truth and made several abortive efforts to escape, sails a small boat to the horizon, which turns out to be a *trompe l'oeil* scrim easily pierced by his prow. The show's 'creator' gives him one last chance to stay, but that he cannot do.[2] *Dark City* hero John Murdoch discovers the Shell Beach of his supposed childhood memories is nothing but a billboard pasted over a brick wall – which, when breached, reveals the 'city' to be floating in space.

The Thirteenth Floor is the most reflexive and also the most flatfooted of these stories, which makes it particularly useful as a reference: no allegories here, and little imagination to obscure the Ideas. In the denouement, Douglas Hall[3] simply crests a hill to discover that what he had thought was the real world has, beyond this point, yet to be constructed. In lieu of landscape, only crude phosphor-green polygons: the basic units of video graphics rendering, in the primal monochrome of an old CRT.

The raw material of the simulation is even more basic in *The Matrix* – machine language itself, in the same familiar green, which must be translated and translated again to produce the virtual reality occupying the minds of passive humans.

That colour is one of the few archaicisms *The Matrix* allows itself – a rarity that is itself unusual. Edge of the Construct films prefer to set their constructs in the past, perhaps for reasons no more mysterious than the ways in which memory is itself a kind of virtual reality. Truman's town is spiffily late-1950s, *Dark City* presents a pointedly motley but largely 40s noir metropolis, and *The Thirteenth Floor* programmers have recreated 1937 Los Angeles.

Only *The Matrix* sets its sim in the present, parallel to the movie's making. 'You believe it's the year 1999 when in fact it's closer to 2199,' says Morpheus, charged with explaining things both to Neo and to us. But long before specifying dates, the film flashes enough signs to set the clock

The edge of the construct. Above: *The Truman Show* (Paramount Pictures, 1998).
Bottom: *Dark City* (New Line Productions / New Line Cinema / Mystery Clock Productions, 1998)

right: minidiscs and industrial dance-metal, FedEx uniforms and polyvinyl couture, and the sort of work cubicle that subdivided the age. So it seems reasonable to hope that *The Matrix* might provide the most immediate answers to the question of why, exactly, this kind of story was so prevalent, over the course of fifteen months at the end of the 20th century.

What is the Matrix?

The Matrix is grounded in two science fiction commonplaces: the war between man and machine, and the possibility that reality is a hoax.[4] These clichés are not the film's plot; they simply set the terms for it. The early portion of the story is summarised, with only a bit of exaggeration, by Agent

Top: *The Thirteenth Floor* (Centropolis Entertainment / 13th Floor Productions Inc. / Filmstifung Nordrhein-Westfalen, 1999)

Smith (Hugo Weaving), after he has arrested Neo at the office where he works:

As you can see, we've had our eye on you for some time now, Mr Anderson. It seems that you've been living two lives. In one life, you're Thomas A. Anderson, program writer for a respectable software company, you have a social security number, you pay your taxes, and you help your landlady carry out her garbage. The other life is lived in computers, where you go by the hacker alias Neo and are guilty of virtually every computer crime we have a law for. One of these lives has a future, and one of them does not. I'm going to be as forthcoming as I can be, Mr Anderson. You're here because we need your help. We know that you've been contacted by a certain individual, a man who calls himself Morpheus. Now whatever you think you know about this man is irrelevant. He is considered by many authorities to be the most dangerous man alive.

What Smith doesn't know is that Neo has already had a nightclub flirtation with Morpheus's lieutenant Trinity (Carrie-Anne Moss), whom we know from the astonishing fight'n'flight sequence that opens the film. Though they fail to 'meet cute', their brief exchange is Neo's leap toward waking; it's also sexy. 'I know why you hardly sleep,' the vinyl-clad Trinity breathes into his ear, 'why you live alone, and why night after night you sit at your computer.' How indissoluble are desire for consciousness and consciousness of desire! But Neo is reminded that his solitary quest is not really for another:

TRINITY: It's the question that drives us mad. It's the question that brought you here. You know the question just as I did.
NEO: What is the Matrix?

In fairly short order, Neo is bugged by the Agents; debugged by Trinity and her companions Apoc and Shift; and led to a meeting with Morpheus, who offers the now-famous[5] choice:

Unfortunately, no one can be told what the Matrix is. You have to see it for yourself. This is your last chance. After this there is no turning back. You take the blue pill, the story ends, you wake up in your bed and believe whatever you want to believe. You take the red pill, you stay in Wonderland, and I show you how deep the rabbit hole goes – remember, all I'm offering is the truth, nothing more.

As is so often the case, the truth is chatty. The speeches begin even before Neo's actual body is freed from one of the gooey biomechanical pods in which humans remain suspended, and taken aboard the rebel ship *Nebuchadnezzar*. Morpheus handles most of the soliloquising: the nature of the Matrix; the history of the war between men and machines; the nature of the Matrix; the current struggle between rebels of Zion and their machine oppressors; the nature of the Matrix. Along with this education, Neo receives practical training in becoming a master of the Matrix rather than its slave – training that includes an elegant and discursive slugfest with Morpheus, in a virtual dojo.

This is the second of *The Matrix*'s three major fight sequences; the last and most elaborate waits, naturally, at the film's climax. These fights isolate the movie's three sections: that before Neo's awakening from the Matrix; that in which Neo, with the help of friends, comes to understand the Matrix; and that in which Neo and friends return superhero-style to kick some ass in the Matrix. Put another way, the film's three parts are *preconscious*, *conscious* and *superconscious*.

The second section ends with Neo's visit to 'The Oracle' (Gloria Foster), where his messianic potential is assessed (a deceptive 'sorry, kiddo') and a couple of Philosophy 101 topics are bandied about. From this point on, *The Matrix* gives itself to the roller-coaster action most patrons must have been expecting when they queued for tickets. Betrayed by one of their own, the crew of the *Neb* suffers several casualties; Morpheus is captured. The Agents, led as always by Smith, hope to gain from him access codes to Zion's mainframe computer, allowing the crushing of the rebellion. Morpheus is rescued in the nick of time – at the price of Neo's life. Miraculously, a kiss from Trinity restores him. In the final scene he steps from a phone booth, slips on his mirrorshades, and rockets into the sky.

Liberal Arts

Whatever the Matrix is, *The Matrix* is a movie. It's a visual object, and much of its meaning must reside there. It's also a significant event in the history of film – its industry, its audience – and this too demands an account. But, inescapably, it's a movie that alternately whispers and bellows its possession of Big Ideas; to ignore these cries would be as foolish as to accept them without question.

There have already been a number of books and countless articles more or less devoted to, as one title bluntly offers, *The Matrix and Philosophy*. These works tend to be fascinated, in fact, with both philosophy and theology; the film doesn't shy from proffering fuel for both fires. The religious tracts follow two main paths: the messianic features Neo as the One who will save humans from their enslavement by the machines; the Gnostic rehearses the worldview in which humans are prevented from realising heaven through the elaborate deception of a malevolent demiurge.

This latter structure, so familiar to sci-fi fans from Philip K. Dick tales and the movies that love them,[6] dovetails graciously with the most popular of the philosophical investigations: the 'brain in a vat' hypothesis.[7] It takes the form of the basic epistemological conjecture described by Jonathan Dancy: 'You do not know that you are not a brain, suspended in a vat full of liquid in a laboratory, and wired to a computer which is feeding you your current experiences under the control of some ingenious technician scientist.'

The reader will perhaps be happy to learn that I plan to take up these questions only in order to set them immediately aside. This is not to deny their presence. In one of their relatively rare interviews, the writer-directors (Larry and Andy Wachowski) responded to a question about how much of the religious and philosophical reference was intentional with a terse 'All of it.'[8] Such concerns are compelling, especially if you're stoned. However, they're so general they could attach to many films and almost any time. As noted earlier, the 'brain in a vat' hypothesis in particular is essentially a variation on the *reality is a hoax* or *it could all be a dream* imaginary – a veritable sci-fi cliché.[9]

If we accept that the movie is more interesting than the cliché, we're left wondering why so many commentators settle on readings of such banality. The first answer must be that the film so demands: The screenplay and scenario studiously invite us to grow entangled in their conceptions, their insights and meanderings, *as if we were characters*. But in so doing, we risk losing track of the film as a total object, as a cultural product of its time and place. We give ourselves to understanding the Matrix, rather than *The Matrix*.

Moreover, I would suggest that theology and analytic philosophy here are equally convivial sorts of inverted belletrism, promising a moral or instructive content while requiring little but passive contemplation. The former provides not reference so much as the *sensation of reference*, the satisfaction of catching at least some of the allusions as they pass by, like watching *Jeopardy* or reading *Foucault's Pendulum*. And the latter, similarly, provides the *sensation of abstract thinking*.

What's obscured by these satisfactions is, to put it in the terms of the film, real life: all that might be concerned with the nuts and bolts of everyday existence, and all that might speak to actual social relations in specific moments. In a word, history.

It's a messy category, resistant to the transcendental longueurs of messianism and metaphysics. And it certainly won't explain everything – nor does it wish to. I accept that *The Matrix* is a kitchen sink running over with ideas great and small, often tossed in with more concern for their cool-appeal than their coherence; I have seen the sequels. Certainly, it's tempting, given that this is not *Antigone* but a Hollywood blockbuster, to assume that it wishes to be all things to everyone – or at least enough things to enough people that its owners, having blown $60 million, might reap the whirlwind.

But if denying the movie its particularities by settling for passive and abstract meanings is an easy out, dismissing the film's capacity to have meanings beyond its entertainment value is equally lazy. Signing the dismissal slip with the name 'incoherence' ought to make us especially leery.

History is not coherent; moreover, the politics of coherence tend to drive history in the least tolerable directions. So again, since we are still in the Introduction – a calm moment for averrals and caveats – I'll accept that *The Matrix* will fail any test for coherence. Indeed, it flickers under the sign of two contradictions, which correspond to its paired sci-fi commonplaces. It's a historic advance in digital entertainment that is unpacifiably anxious about the dangers of digitality; it's a critique of spectacles that is itself a spectacle. These two pairs organise the central four chapters of this book.

If the movie is contradictory, this may not be at odds with the audience's ambivalences about its own experiences outside the theatre. And if the film's ideas fail to form some totality, they might still be partial to something rather specific, and rather evident. I want to propose that, if there is an allegory to be found in *The Matrix*, it's not about truth. Equally, though it might concern these things, it's not about machines, nor is it about movies. It's about life as we lived it around 1999.

Long before that threshold, Marshall McLuhan proposed that there were two kinds of media: 'light on' and 'light through'. The latter included the most longstanding forms: paintings, the newspaper, street signs. The former suggests more modern apparitions: movies, television, computer screens. This distinction is nowhere more vivid than in the wired cubicle of 1999, shaded on three sides by temporary partitions and on the fourth opening into a labyrinth of more cubicles, each with a monitor rather than a window – a country in which *light through* had displaced *light on* with imperial indifference.

For billions of people, this was not a central story of 1999. But for the core audience of *The Matrix*, daily life bobbed near the wavefront of the tech boom, the infinitely expanding 'new economy' that was always hiring, if you could write code or just punch keys. You worked in a cubicle not so different from Thomas Anderson's, for a company that wanted as many of your hours as it could get, and had newer and better ways to get them. Everything was fluid but the work. The company might change every month, and the cubicle needn't be fixed. Any monitor would do, if it could connect to the system. At stake is not whether this was good or bad, but rather simply that it was, at that moment, a social fact. You sat at a workstation and worked long hours staring at a screen. When you were done, if you weren't too exhausted, maybe you went to the movies.

2 Good Digital

Nothing is true. Everything is permitted.

Last words of Rashid al-Din Sinan

The Matrix waits three minutes before stopping the show. Trapped by four policemen in room 303 of the derelict Heart O' the City Hotel, Trinity has already disarmed the first officer to approach.[10] She then leaps improbably high into the air, assuming an exaggerated martial arts pose while rising. Suddenly the camera whirls 180 degrees around their suspended forms, in a continuous motion from one profile view to the other; the dowdy cop is frozen, while the fetish-wear freedom fighter ascends a few more increments. Time has stopped for everyone but her.

But of course it's for her that time has stopped – that is, it waits while she gathers herself. For the moment she's time's master; she seems to have a gentleman's agreement with gravity as well. Then, just as suddenly as it abdicated, real time (at least *The Matrix*'s version of it) resumes its rightful authority. Trinity caroms the first cop into a second, then kicks a chair across the room to disable a third. The rebel without a pause runs up and along one wall and accelerates onto another – eluding gunfire all the while – before descending to grab the fourth cop and use his pistol (still in hand) to blow away the third. Finally, she drops the last man standing, positioned behind her as she faces the camera, with a kick over her own shoulder. From first blow to last, the fight is 20 seconds long, a mere three of which are given over to the special effect known as 'bullet time'. Nobody in the audience had ever seen anything like it.

That's not exactly true: it was possible to have seen things *like* it. A lesser version of bullet time, wherein the camera appeared to circle objects and bodies fully stilled in their flight, had already slipped without much notice into a couple other sci-fi movies by way of that nouveau hotbed of cinematic innovation, the commercial spot (in particular, a Smirnoff advert and the better-known 'Khakis Swing' spot for clothiers The Gap).

Seemingly impossible martial arts stunts might have been familiar to fans of Hong Kong pulp cinema – particularly those films that used the device known, for obvious reasons, as 'wire fighting'. This technique would later add supernally elegant chop-socky to Ang Lee's Academy Awarded artpop smash *Crouching Tiger, Hidden Dragon* (2000), which employed legendary Hong Kong choreographer/director Yuen Wo Ping. But it wasn't Ang Lee who first brought Wo Ping to the West; it was the Wachowski Brothers, for *The Matrix*.

They knew what they needed. Subjecting their film to a bit of wry reductivism, Andy Wachowski remarked, 'It's about robots vs. kung fu.' While the category *about* recedes from every director's grasp when the first ticket is sold,[11] this claim has its charms: bullet time and Wo Ping are both hidden within it, equally necessary and complementary elements.

If we manage to focus on Trinity's face in this opening sequence (not an easy task), it's fierce and somewhat pained; her opponents', naturally, grimace and contort as they take their beatings. For the viewer, however, the experience is one of visual delight. This has ever been the root perversity of the movie fight scene – but the distance between these two positions is slighter than it first appears. Both for audiences who love to be amazed, and for film-makers trying to choreograph the same damn fight and make it new, kicks just keep getting harder to find. Thus the brilliance of the scene: while neither element is strictly speaking an innovation, the wedding of bullet time and wire fighting appears as an invention. A little robotics, a little kung fu – a new kick.

Over the course of the film, both techniques will take further star turns, from leaping triple kicks to the visible dodging of bullets.[12] Moreover, the plot designs to render such moments as not being amazing absurdities; we are not asked to suspend our disbelief so much as to understand the terms by which these episodes are believable. This makes them all the more astonishing, since they can't be mentally segregated in the common way SFX set pieces are understood to exist as self-justifying thrills. The narrative doesn't make way for the effects; it demands them.

This makes a divided demand on the audience. On the one hand, the special effects ask us to occupy the same position as the film's sympathetic characters, forcing a dramatic awareness of the degree to

The rules of the game suspended

which images are subject to manipulation in *The Matrix*. Just so, to be human in the Matrix is to be mesmerised by digital fabrication.

On the other hand, such effects render the humans peculiarly insubstantial. The movie is not about them. From the perspective of pleasure, the movie is about digital effects. The assertion that they were the star of the film was common in reviews of the time, and though this was scarcely a new remark (generally an implicit belittlement), it seems in this case particularly apt. Pixar Studios' *Toy Story* (1995) might have been made entirely with digital imaging tech, but *The Matrix* insists on absolute conceptual terms – a digital entertainment about being digital. It is, in its way, a far more loaded foreshadowing of the future of the actorless movie, and the future of Hollywood.

Backstories

That may seem unkind to Keanu Reeves, the once-bankable star who, since *Speed* (1994), had seemingly cast himself from the heights of the A-list. The misses weren't particularly close, either. A movie about the Beats, *The Last Time I Committed Suicide* (1997), scarcely saw the dark of theatres; *Feeling Minnesota* (1996) would have been grateful for such a fate. Reeves's style, a target of occasional mockery when he has passed through the public eye, is famously lacking in affect; moreover, he's suspiciously beautiful. One defence of his acting technique, taking into account the latter debilitation, runs, 'It's not easy to let the camera just look at you.'

And yet, whether it's the swift and requisite reaction shots of action films, or the languorous lens of Gus Van Sant in *My Own Private Idaho* (1991), surely one should betray something. Reeves's reactions are so minimal they can verge on the autistic, which sometimes leads to the sensation that his character is simply incapable of registering what's happening to him, or perhaps that his mind is elsewhere. In fact, he's at his most compelling when playing roles dependent on these very circumstances. These include his turn as an inarticulate adolescent in *River's Edge* (1986), utterly outstripped by events; and as the pure product of Southern Californian suburbia in *Bill & Ted's Excellent Adventure*

(1989). Most remarkably and absurdly, he carried the role of Siddhartha for Bernardo Bertolucci in *Little Buddha* (1993). Zen quips about emptiness, and being of 'no mind', were not lost to the critical record.

No scenario held more promise for his signature style than *Johnny Mnemonic*, the 1995 flop that would be remembered as a disaster were it memorable at all. William Gibson wrote the screenplay from his own (quite different) short story, doubly intertwining the film with the heritage of *The Matrix*: not just as a Keanu prelude, but as the first story brought to screen from the progenitor of the cyberpunk genre.[13] Though Gibson's novels have proved notoriously resistant to adaptation, he stands alongside Philip K. Dick as the author casting the longest shadow on Hollywood's future-fictions.[14]

This would be the case were we to consider only Gibson's transformative debut *Neuromancer*, which as early as 1986 envisioned an immersive 'cyberspace' (as he named it), and imagined it within the context of a dystopian future that pitted humans against a diffuse and concealed Artificial Intelligence.[15] *The Matrix* turns to Gibson again and again, from the vertiginous opening descent through a computer screen into graphical code-land, to the rebel redoubt dubbed Zion, to the film's obsession with eyewear, particularly of the reflective sort.[16] And then there's the film's conceit itself. In the following passage from early in *Neuromancer*, an educational TV show somewhat awkwardly bears the expositional weight:

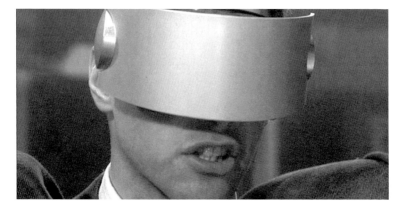

Information worker Johnny Mnemonic's blank stare (*Johnny Mnemonic*, Alliance Communications Corporation, 1995)

'The matrix has its roots in primitive arcade games,' said the voice-over, 'in early graphics programs and military experimentation with cranial jacks.' On the Sony, a two-dimensional space war faded behind a forest of mathematically generated ferns, demonstrating the spatial possibilities of logarithmic spirals – cold blue military footage burned through, lab animals wired into test systems, helmets feeding into fire control circuits of tanks and war planes. 'Cyberspace. A consensual hallucination experienced daily by billions of legitimate operators, in every nation, by children being taught mathematical concepts … A graphic representation of data abstracted from the banks of every computer in the human system.'

This conception preceded the first graphical Web browser by almost a decade. Perhaps even more signally for the genre, *Neuromancer* essentially invented the hacker-as-action hero.

Johnny Mnemonic is no hacker, however. He is a physical labourer, albeit of a peculiar kind, reconceived for the information age. He rents out portions of his brain for the storage and transport of valuable data; he's a hard drive with legs. Significantly, he has no conscious access to the digital data he carries; he's perfectly alienated labour of the digital era.[17] In the story, his goal is to unlock the information before it gets him killed; in the movie, directed by art star Robert Longo, the data has been stored too long and is corrupting his brain. This, surely, is a man with his mind otherwise occupied.

Aside from its casting insight, the film has little to recommend it. Still, it offers a useful way to think about *The Matrix*'s lead, the least actorly of stars. Like Schwarzenegger's Terminator, Keanu Reeves was meant to realise himself as a not-quite-human.[18] But unlike the processed bodybuilder/future Governor, Keanu wasn't quite made to play a machine. With his unassignable looks (often attributed to his genetic heritage of Chinese, Caucasian and Hawaiian) already seeming digitally smoothed, and his immediate proffering of pure surface without depth, he's closer to the dream of a next generation – a post-national, post-modern poster boy. In both appearance and manner, his quality is that of the actor without qualities – the New Star, destined not to distract from the digital *mise en scène* but to integrate with it seamlessly.

Reeves's capacity to occupy the camera's gaze as a sort of passive object – a talent traditionally marked as feminine – suggests an androgyny so often marked next-gen, futuristic. This is underscored by Carrie-Anne Moss, who seems to have been styled (if not indeed cast) for her resemblance to him (in 2003, a *TV Guide* cover would offer a hologram of the kind that shifts images depending on the angle of view, depicting an all-but-indistinguishable Moss and Reeves in their roles for a *Matrix* sequel).[19]

Moreover, the role demands it: for the film's first section, he must appear as appearance itself, a digital projection of a human. This explains not just his image but his affect. With an existence limited to a pod and a

Persons of opposite sex sharing a look

confabulated consciousness, Thomas Anderson lacks real experiences entirely. No wonder he's a man without qualities, lacking interiority. And no sooner is he rescued from these circumstances than he's expected, not to inhabit his humanity, but to exceed it so as to save his kind. Again, experience is loaded directly into his brain – combat training and so forth. 'How is he?' asks Morpheus during the first data session. 'Ten hours straight,' marvels Tank, the crewmember overseeing the process. 'He's a machine.' But of course he's not; he's a vat-grown human who must better the machines at their own game, must be equally at home in the digital and analog worlds. He's the New Man.

Futurama

The New Man is a frontier figure, and his frontier is always the same – he mediates the arrival of the future into the present. If this seems an idea borrowed from theory, it's a theory in which Neo is well versed, to judge from his final soliloquy. 'I know you're out there,' begins his long goodbye:

'I can feel you now. I know that you're afraid. You're afraid of us. You're afraid of change. I don't know the future. I didn't come here to tell you how this is going to end. I came here to tell you how it's going to begin.

This might simply be his way of warning us that sequels are forthcoming. But it's also a promise that the film is not a vision of the future, but a start to it – a promise the film endeavours to keep. *The Matrix*'s profound influence on visual culture meant that a broad swath of popular culture would bear the marks of its futurism forward – from clothing fashions to car commercials, mobile phones to political leaflets.

Nowhere did the visuals have a bigger impact than on films themselves; Neo's monologue might as well have been directed at the guild. By the next year, the ubiquity of *Matrix* effects, particularly when unmotivated by the script, was already a form of Hollywood self-ironising. When *Charlie's Angels* (2000) unleashed the bullet-time/wire-fighting combination, we were meant to chuckle as much as to marvel. By 2003,

The New Yorker's Anthony Lane would declare, 'What I think of as the "Matrix" shot, a lone figure frozen while the camera travels around him, has traveled quickly from novelty to cliché.'

What surprises Lane is that the effect has trickled down from the Hollywood blockbuster to a small international film, in that case the Brazilian neo-realist *City of God.* Later in the same year, a lo-rez version of bullet time would structure the DV shorts of Liisa Lounila, Finland's official entry at the Venice Biennale. The traditional story of aesthetic advance proposes that autonomous artists pioneer techniques that will be recuperated in the future by the industrial mainstream.[20] But in this case, time is out of joint. The promise Neo makes within to the film holds equally true for the industry exterior to *The Matrix*; visually, it had arrived at one future first and delivered it to the present.

It is time exactly that is at stake here, and not only in the relationship of present and future. Lane, in the remainder of the passage cited above, defends the effect in question by supplying the director a motivation: 'Meireilles just about keeps it alive by using it to track the passage of time.' But it always did. Bullet time's sublimity, from the moment of Trinity's leap, derives exactly from the way, as I suggested earlier, that it renders unto Caesar what was never Caesar's: control over time itself.

Time mattered in America in 1999 – mattered everywhere, in general, even more than usual. I'll get to that. But in Hollywood, control over time mattered with utter specificity, because of a digital diversion with a ridiculous name.

Game Time

During the last six weeks of 1998 – a rather crucial earning window for the film business – a videogame called *The Legend of Zelda: Ocarina of Time* outearned any Hollywood release. This represented an unprecedented and unexpected development; the home-console gaming world was still in its infancy, relatively speaking. Yet, in 1999 it would almost overtake Hollywood's $7.45 billion income with $6.3 billion of its own; two years later, while Hollywood posted a record year at $8.35 billion domestic, the fledgling gamebiz waved from the passing lane en route to $9.4 billion.

These were the numbers of the times, but also the signs. The videogame's ascendancy was irrevocably writ into the tech boom: it was new, it was interactive, it was a gizmo. Whether one played on a PC or a dedicated platform like PlayStation or GameCube, it was, in fact, a computer – fully digital, all code.[21] Movies were so Twentieth Century, so *analog*.

Hollywood understood the challenge, as it has mostly understood such insults to its supremacy, as something to be assimilated. Sometimes this looked quite a bit like bowing and scraping, as with the run of mostly embarrassing flicks based on popular gaming titles.[22] These films were bad not because they failed the standards of the cinema, but because they misrecognised the terrain of the competition itself: immersivity. That somewhat nebulous term of art describes the extent to which a videogame draws players into its world, so they feel interior to it rather than being a passive, exterior observer. Immersion experiences are typically recounted in terms of time – generally how we lose track of it, how its motion seems diverted from the daily tick-tock.

It's possible to conceive of *The Matrix* as in many ways a response to the challenge of videogaming. It remains a movie – no joystick. But looking at, for example, bullet time, we recognise it as an explicit immersion effect. Shot from our point of view, the optical perspective swoops through a three-dimensional space, fully-rendered, 360 degrees, without ever revealing the apparatus of film-making; we could be inside the synthworld of *Zelda*, except that the graphics are incomparably higher resolution. Real, more or less. And even better: we can dodge bullets.

This is the extraordinary advance in *The Matrix*'s version of bullet time. If everything stops while the camera wheels around the scene (as in 'Khaki Swing'), we're still watching objects, still outside as analytic viewers. It's perhaps like Eadweard Muybridge's stroboscopic photos of a man running, except it's the body that's still, the camera shifting incrementally. Then again, it's something like Cubism, pictorially revealing all perspectives of a still life on a two-dimensional surface.

However, if the scene is frozen *but the hero can move through it* – if all the power and agency is vested in a singular figure with which we have

identified – the circumstances resemble those of a videogame as extensively as a movie can, and still be a movie. For the duration, we have the masterful relation to time already enjoyed by every videogamer.[23] Inevitably, then, the featured bullet-time sequences of *The Matrix* echo the most popular combat formats of videogames: martial arts and the shooter. In combination with wire fighting, the physics-defying moves of videogames become available to the screen as well.

If that weren't enough, the movie's story presents its own technologies according to the structures of the videogame. The 'loading program' is, in effect, a videogame into which the rebels jack: as Morpheus explains, 'We can load anything from clothing, to equipment,

The digital dojo

Top: *Mortal Kombat: Deception* (Midway Amusement Games, LLC, 2004). Below: *Mortal Kombat: Deadly Alliance* (Midway Amusement Games, LLC, 2002)

weapons, training simulations, anything we need.' Shortly, Neo tries the jump program and then the sparring program; his epic fight with Morpheus replicates game combat so exquisitely it could rightly be considered an homage to the competition.

Shortly thereafter, Morpheus will lead Neo through a scenario involving Agents and a woman in a red dress: 'another training program'. The youngest crewmember[24] Mouse will later tell Neo, 'You know, I wrote that program … The woman in the red dress? I designed her. She, um … well she doesn't talk very much, but … but if you'd like to meet her, I can arrange a much more personalised meeting.' Beyond the surface comedy of digital libido (itself no stranger to gamers), the movie makes the chain of logic clear: the videogame is a digitally falsified reality, but is also the form of entertainment proper to programmers, whose power lies exactly in that they might be authors of that reality. The quotation from Gibson now seems a double entendre: *The matrix has its roots in primitive arcade games.* Moreover, skills are delivered to Neo's brain exactly the way *Virtua Fighter* is delivered to a monitor: via the slotting of data cartridge into console. And the results are the same: a dazed guy, just hours ago a mere cubicle worker, snaps out of an immersion trance and exclaims (in perhaps the film's most adolescent moment) 'I know kung fu!'

If *The Matrix* merely deployed digital effects in a way particularly resonant for gamers, there would be little to do but salute its technical virtuosity and marketing acumen, and move on. If only anxiety were so easy to manage. Instead, the surpassing power of digital immersion becomes the central concern of the film itself. As suggested earlier, the special effects cannot be extricated from the narrative, from the movie's worldview. Indeed, it might be argued that, taken in sum, the effects *are* the worldview: there is a digital confabulation. It is thrilling, and filled with visual pleasure, and designed to surround one's consciousness utterly. The particular consciousness toward which the effects are directed is that of a tech worker, who of course imagines himself as a stylish, cutting-edge hacker.

It becomes difficult to discern whether this forms a description of audience and film, or of Neo and the Matrix. This isn't a confusion, nor a reflexive metafilmic device. Or rather it is, but it is also what allows the movie to be about something beyond itself. The endless confusion of insides and outsides lets us fall quite far into the story. It also allows the story to flow in a peristaltic action out to the world beyond the theatre door. Mediating relentlessly between the present and the future, analog and digital, *The Matrix* could lay claim to being the most immersive movie ever made; it was without question the movie most haunted by the fear of immersion.

3 Bad Digital

But certainly for the present age, which prefers the sign to the thing signified, the copy to the original, representation to the reality, the appearance to the essence ... illusion only is *sacred*, truth *profane*.

Feuerbach, *The Essence of Christianity*

Put another way, if *The Matrix* revels in the immersive possibilities of digital pleasures, the Matrix is a terror of digital immersion; this leaves the film as an ambivalent object, shuddering between positions in a kind of delirium.

The story trumps the solipsistic paranoias of some other Edge of the Construct films; the captive and misled heroes in *The Truman Show* or *Dark City* are allowed at least to have bodies. In those scenarios, the material world itself must be changed (as with a film set) to maintain the enclosing and falsified reality. In *The Matrix*, the lie is poured directly into the brain. In the words of Slavoj Žižek, it proffers 'the radical reduction of the wealth of our sensory experiences to – not even letters, but – the minimal digital series of 0 and 1, of passing and non-passing of the electrical signal'.[25]

To engage fully with this fear, we must tarry with the real. Žižek, the psychoanalytically trained theorist, opens the talk from which the above quote was taken with a sardonic description of seeing the film with 'the perfect audience', which turns out to be 'an idiot. A man in his late twenties was so immersed in the film that he all the time disturbed the other spectators with loud exclamations, like 'My God, wow, there is no reality!'' Better such idiocy, Žižek suggests, than being suckered into finding something deeper in the movie, which he delimits as

one of the few films which function as a kind of Rorschach test, like the proverbial painting of God which seems always to stare directly at you, from wherever you look at it: practically every theoretical orientation seems to recognize itself in it.[26]

The critic here strikes a strange pose, given his own propensity for recognising *Jacques Lacan in Hollywood* (as one of his books is called).[27]

Žižek essentially offers the audience two roles (other than that of mute spectator): idiots and pseudo-intellectuals. One can imagine this satisfying a Hollywood producer; it's a cheerful demographic vision, from the seller's perspective. Žižek is happy to play both parts. Not only has he published his psychoanalytic study of the film, but he's speculated about the film's reality question, as declaimed by Morpheus:

What is real? How do you define real? If you're talking about what you can feel, what you can smell, what you can taste and see, then real is simply electrical signals interpreted by your brain. This is the world that you know. The world as it was at the end of the twentieth century. It exists now only as part of a neural-interactive simulation that we call the Matrix. You've been living in a dream world, Neo. This is the world as it exists today. Welcome to the Desert of the Real.

Inside the film, evidently, the question is answered almost as soon as it is asked. Žižek nonetheless forecast that the film's 'reality' (Zion, the *Nebuchadnezzar*, the blackened earth *circa* 2199) would be itself revealed as the next Matrix, the next level of falsification.[28] But, as noted, the recursive revelation that we have again not woken into real reality is a commonplace of such genre films. It might be more useful to wonder why we care about *the real* in the first place. Given the film's ambivalence – the extent to which it retails digital technology as the source of its very existence, and of our pleasure – we see that it proposes a problem more complex than concerns about vats and brains. The anxiety isn't about the real, but about what our relationship to the real should be. Or, just as passionately per the predilections of postmodernism, what our relationship to the fake should be. Another way of initiating the same curiosity would be to ask why, exactly, superstar postmodernists like Slavoj Žižek come to devote themselves to speculating about a popular movie?

The Phrase that Concerns Us

Because they have been sent an invitation. Every letter, they say, reaches its destination; in *The Matrix*, the first missive is a brief shot of a book. This occurs during a sequence wherein friends drop by to purchase something illicit, something stored on a minidisc that Neo has in turn stashed inside said book, hollowed out for that very purpose.

The entire scene howls with an excess of significance – especially during a second viewing. It opens with drowsing Neo awoken[29] by his computer, and contacted for the first time by the rebels. This chat leads directly to a knock on the door (numbered 101, natch) from Neo's client Choi, who, grateful to pay $2,000 for whatever's on the disc, professes, 'Hallelujah. You're my saviour, man. My own personal Jesus Christ.' Neo, curbing his friend's enthusiasm, warns him, 'You get caught using that … ', to which Choi avers, 'Yeah, I know. This never happened. You don't exist.' Moments later, he offers, 'Hey, it just sounds to me like you need to unplug, man.' And so on, one oblivious double entendre after the next, through the Lewis Carroll moment when Neo follows the 'white rabbit' – a tattoo on the shoulder of Choi's partner DuJour – down the hole of the plot.

In the midst of all this referential mania, the most loaded image remains the disc in the gutted book. It reflects exactly Žižek's inverted hierarchy, wherein the stark purity of binary code has replaced 'even letters' in the depths of the irreal. The written word, that messy analog dataform, has been summarily discarded. Or, even more anxiously, the book form survives as nothing but a shell; it exists only to conceal a more powerful form of data, and to mask its own absence. The little invention is a perfect symbol for the procession of simulacra; we can see how such a set piece is, among other things, a seduction of theory.

The seducer can never rest, however, until the seduction is complete; more mash notes are required. As every graduate student with a pause button on their DVD remote is by now aware, the empty book in question is *Simulacra & Simulation* (in an austere if anomalously thick clothbound edition lacking the author's name) by the clown prince of post-modernism, Jean Baudrillard. Camp followers of the cultural-theoretical complex would shortly learn, via glossy magazine interviews, that the Brothers Wachowski had given the book to Reeves in preparation for the role. This itself was a curiosity, as telling a moment in the popularisation of pomo theory as *The Matrix* itself: Jean Baudrillard's name cropping up routinely in celebrity profiles on the cologned pages of *Details* and *Rolling Stone*.[30]

It's worth considering some of Baudrillard's ideas, not only because of how insistently the film would like us to, but because he has clearly lavished considerable attention on the issue of simulation, on occasion within the context of Hollywood. In the book at hand, he recounts Borges's tale of a country that buries its territory under a perfect 1:1 scale map, which by the end has begun to fray and disintegrate, 'a few shreds still discernible in the deserts'.

This seems like a useful parable for the order of *The Matrix*, with its synthetic reality perfectly concealing the original. But already the comparison starts to fail. In the movie's plot, it's the real world that's in tatters, while the Matrix of pure information remains intact, gleaming, realer than real. This is exactly what Baudrillard foresaw:

[I]f we were to revive the fable today, it would be the territory whose shreds are slowly rotting across the map. It is the real, and not the map, whose vestiges subsist here and there, in the deserts which are no longer those of the Empire, but our own. *The desert of the real itself.*

The italics are the author's; he has saved the Wachowski Brothers the trouble. W recognise the language from the phrase employed by Morpheus to introduce to his charge the plot's big truth.[31] The film, moreover, now seems perfectly explicit in its borrowing. When Morpheus intones 'this is the world you know', he gestures toward a series of images on a television screen – the synthetic version, the map, as it were – and these retain their coherent sheen. When his soliloquy arrives at its bottom line, 'the world as it exists today', he and Neo plummet vertiginously into the world as it is, the territory: a ruined landscape.

The real isn't what it used to be. Again, we must credit Baudrillard, who seems not only to have ghost-directed the scenario but to have considered the film in full sixteen years in advance of its premiere:

When the real is no longer what it used to be, nostalgia assumes its full meaning. There is a proliferation of myths of origin and signs of reality ... there is a panic stricken production of the real and the referential, above and parallel to the panic of material production: this is how simulation appears in the phase that concerns us.

The French philosopher and the Hollywood film differ in their suppositions only as to the right *now*, the moment when reality has collapsed and nostalgia assumed its full meaning. For the sake of some contingent stability, I want to return to the idea that the now at stake isn't the movie's 2199, nor Baudrillard's 1983, but 1999. But then we must ask: whose 1999? Agent Smith will clarify that this date was chosen as the arbitrary present of the simulation after a first draft of the Matrix failed. Initially 'designed to be a perfect human world', perfection turned out not to be persuasive, and people kept waking up from it – a failure of immersivity, one might say. 'Which is why the Matrix was redesigned to this: the peak of your civilisation.' The film's 1999 is the good ol' days, before the bottom fell out of the reality market: the present we are nostalgic *for*.

Baudrillard diagnoses nostalgia as a sense that rises as reality recedes, and then describes the symptoms in terms that might as well be a blurb for

the movie. '[A] proliferation of myths of origin and signs of reality' compacts the metaphysical and theological vagaries into a single phrase, while 'a panic stricken production of the real and the referential' might as well be the film's subtitle (if only we lived in a world where Sorbonne profs were Hollywood players[32]). These phrases don't describe the world within the film, but the film itself; it's not the Matrix that is nostalgic, but *The Matrix*. Baudrillard's reasoning, which the film is so delighted to invoke, demands that it's not the future where reality has run dry, but the present. The film projects its signifying whirlpool two centuries ahead, but can't elude its own material existence; it can't be a symptom of a different time. Our 1999 is the phase that concerns us, the present we are nostalgic *in*.

'Welcome to the desert of the real'

Strange Days Indeed

Nostalgia is of considerable interest to *The Matrix*, though it plays only a small role in the characters' emotional lives (its solitary appearance in the film informs Cypher's decision to betray the revolution; he misses the taste of steak). Living in the past bears the same relation to the real as does living in a simulation. It's a false consciousness, but as long as that indwelling is imperfect, incomplete – identifiably irreal – it should establish the reality of what's found beyond itself. The present is real because nostalgia isn't, built as it is of partial and fading memories.

But the moment that nostalgia becomes total – as immediate and encompassing as the present – it can no longer secure the present's reality (this goes a long way toward explaining why Edge of the Construct movies tend to set their illusory but totally realised worlds in the past). *Strange Days* (1995) takes this up with gracious directness; uncoincidentally, it recognises the threat as digitality itself. A crime thriller directed by Kathryn Bigelow,[33] it sets itself in the near future: the last hours of 1999. Naturally. The crime at its heart is the arbitrary execution of a militant rap star by the Los Angeles Police Department during a traffic stop – a shooting perchance recorded by an onlooker. Lenny Nero (Ralph Fiennes), ex-cop and now a dealer, has come into possession of this recording, though for a good while he doesn't know it; meanwhile, various parties pursue it lest it become public and the city go up in flames.

The illicit product Lenny Nero vends – and, as tradition mandates, is himself hooked on – is 'playback': digital recordings of people's lives. The film's singular futuristic gesture is a device called a 'SQUID', which stores everything its wearer sees and experiences. Another person, armed with matching equipment, might later inhabit this recorded consciousness sensation for sensation: a total digital recreation.

Strange Days renders its digital immersion with extended point-of-view shots for which they designed and built a special camera, just as bullet time is a visual analogy for privileged moments of consciousness within the Matrix. This is scarcely the only intersection between the films: as art historians say when dodging claims of actual influence, the two are 'deeply connected'. The SQUID, a 'Superconducting QUantum Interference

Device', is itself taken from the Gibson story 'Johnny Mnemonic'. Like Johnny himself, it's a memory device – but it doesn't store the encrypted data of Japanese gangsters. It stores digitised memories themselves; as it happens, it files them on minidiscs.[34] Perhaps this is exactly what Neo has for Choi, tucked where Baudrillard used to be.

Lenny Nero isn't particularly interested in other people's recordings, other than as objects of commerce. He watches instead his own memories, of his happy life with ex-girlfriend Faith – watches them obsessively and pathetically. He's the very image of nostalgia. But then, the man lost in his memories is a Hollywood type par excellence. Notable here is the

Neo and Nero (bottom: *Strange Days*, Lightstorm Entertainment, 1995) sell some simulation

technologised quality of the nostalgia, of Nero's lostness. Guardian angel Mace (Angela Bassett), in love with Lenny, makes the inevitable speech: 'This is your life, right here, right now. It's real time, you hear me? Real time! … These are used emotions; it's time to trade them in. Memories were meant to fade. They're designed that way for a reason.' Sometimes there is little to do with the explicit but celebrate it.

Strange Days can't be construed as an Edge of the Construct film: there's never any doubt where reality lies, nor is there any superfiction being perpetrated on our hero. Moreover, the movie is more directly a fantasy version, a re-remembering, of the 1991 beating of Rodney King at the hands of the LAPD, and ensuing events. In case this eludes us, the film climaxes with three uniformed officers, cheered on by a colleague, beating and kicking Mace as she writhes on the ground, repeating (as she just had to a captive cop) the all-too-familiar command 'Stay down!'[35]

Still, there's something to be learned by deploying the two heroes adjacently, as if they weren't in that position already. Each in his own 1999, each a consumer of a digital fantasy he must exit to achieve his real life, Nero and Neo confront each other from opposite sides of the mirror.[36] The gulf between them is no broader than the fact that Nero enters and exits his construct out of something like free will, or at least the will enslaved only to sad, human desire. Neo doesn't even know he's living in the past. But Lenny doesn't know that his 'playback' is one movie away from being the Matrix, his 'real time' on the eve of becoming an all-encompassing fantasia.

Nostalgia and simulation are the same problem. Once upon a time, they secured the real through their very falseness, their immateriality. But once under the sign of digitality, they threaten the reality of the real. They are no longer provisional interiors, outside which the real world holds its ground; like the perfect map, they utterly occupy the territory.[37]

This returns us to the image of the disc inside the book, but with its generously straightforward hierarchy disturbed. I took it before as offering an order of simulation that increased the further in one ventured. The figure ought by rights to establish the reality of that which is outside it. Alas. Like Thomas Anderson himself, the book is, after all, nested itself

'Stay down!' Cinematic memory and the nightmare of history (*Strange Days*, the assault on Rodney King, filmed by George Holliday, 3 March 1991)

within a work of code, merely a figment of the Matrix (we can be certain that this, if nothing else, would delight its author). Instability of meanings, collapse of symbolic orders, dissolution of reference frames: this what you get from perfect duplication. Things fall apart, the outside cannot hold.

Todayland

The vertigo of duplication is definitive of the movie; that vertigo is the central sensation of art in the age of digital reproduction. It offers a sequence of confusions: which 1999 are we talking about, which digital spectacle? This in turn leads toward the incessant work of clarification, as we try to discuss the movie: *our* 1999, the *film's* nostalgia, not the Matrix but *The Matrix*.

It is the movie that asks this labour of us. On whose behalf does it ask?

This requires a final voyage with Baudrillard, from the desert to Disneyland. Disneyland is a little primitive, but it's the simulation we know.[38] Within its 'play of illusions and phantasms', one might find an order not so different from America, about which the theorist notes, '[a]ll its values are exalted here, in miniature and comic strip form.' But Baudrillard doesn't settle for arguing that the inside, under cover of its own falsity, is covertly real as the outside. Instead, he offers the reverse – that inside and outside are equally illusory. The Magic Kingdom is visibly fake so that upon exiting, we will believe we have entered a real republic: 'Disneyland is presented as an imaginary in order to make us believe the rest is real, when in fact all of Los Angeles and the America surrounding it are no longer real.'[39]

One sees how Žižek might have come by his suspicion that the movie's narrative exterior, 2199's desert of the real, is another Matrix – that its reality is a seeming, established only by the interior 1999's irreality. But we ourselves are forced into a more uncomfortable position by this constellation. Our interior is that of the film, the theatre. The film has been a simulation; it's made simulation its immediate concern. It's persuaded us to italicise the distinction between its confabulated world and our actual one, to assert our world's reality by parsing the imaginary of the film. Exiting the theatre, it's we who confront the Disneyland problem in spades, we who must worry about never coming to the edge of the construct.

Here we might finally lose the real, by way of the same coup cutting us loose from the fake. All its formulations – simulation, the map, the virtual, nostalgia – stand here for the same shape. The false isn't the problem in and of itself; fear lies in the threat that it might colonise every fold of consciousness. Digitality is relevant exactly insofar as it brings close the possibility of perfectable immersion; as the prospect nears, the threat of immersion becomes intolerable. No wonder *The Matrix* takes a wildly ambivalent stance in relation. Digitech, that is to say, is a medium; it allows one both to image and to imagine an all-encompassing spectacle. But what it mediates is the human experience of such an encompassing, what I'll call totality. It's the totality itself that finally concerns us. That, and what such a totality allows.

Again we must be grateful for the explicit. The false totality called the Matrix – and this throws a sharp light on the irrelevance of most philosophical glosses of the film – hasn't been devised because fooling humans makes for a good time on a Friday night. That would explain only the first portion of the film's expositional bottom line, as explained (inevitably) by Morpheus. 'I came to realise the obviousness of the truth. What is the Matrix? Control. The Matrix is a computer-generated dream world, …' he supposes. So far so good for the brain-in-vat theorists, as long as nobody worries about the category of purpose, of loss and gain. But Morpheus is everready with what they would call the teleology, not

No one is without a little power

even pausing for a new sentence: … 'built to keep us under control in order to change a human being into this'.

At least in this moment we understand why Shift refers to pre-pill Neo as 'coppertop'. But at best, this gesture drags the plot out of abstraction – and explains why Neo has such an exaggerated reaction. Previous unconcealings about vat-grown babies feeding on liquefied corpses have been met with disbelief and growing horror; the glimpse of a Duracell sends Neo into a staggering panic of denial. 'No. I don't believe it … Stop. Let me out. Let me out! I want out!'

Laurence Fishburne, over a discussion of the script's philosophical scope, told me he'd mused plenty in his life about 'all that, you know, spiritual fucking voodoo fucking mumbo jumbo kind of shit' (2003). For him, the religious reading wasn't the film's hard core. As he phrased it, 'The idea that machines are using us for batteries is pretty fucking severe.' The war of man and machine comes not from natural antagonism, nor vaguely presumed will to power. It comes from specific, material needs. The humans have energy. The machines need it. How to get the maximum without facing revolution? That is the question.

But we have a question pending. If Disneyland asks us to notice its irreality on behalf of America, it seems clear *The Matrix* asks us to notice its own irreality on behalf of the same. If I haven't made it clear, the film isn't just about 1999 but about America, the one we entered after leaving the cinema. The movie is a story about individuals dramatically exiting (or failing to exit) into their own lives; the deep hook requires us finding our own story there.

Seen from this perspective, *The Matrix* (along with its companions at the Edge of the Construct) is no more a film of anxiety than of wish fulfilment, in which the frightening phantasm of simulation is balanced by the fantasy of reaching its frontier. This is the wish that so persistently compelled our interest during the period in question, densely and redundantly. We must have suspected that there was no exit, that we might already be inside something from which we might not be able to escape.

4 Good Spectacle

The house was quiet and the world was calm.
The reader became the book; and summer night
Was like the conscious being of the book.

Wallace Stevens, 'The House Was Quiet and the World Was Calm'

To say *The Matrix* was everywhere one turned in 1999 is to say only that it was a popular culture phenomenon. This is the goal toward which every Hollywood film is released – a desire not always fulfilled, but so urgent and ubiquitous that it often has consequences for the thematic structure of the script, whether in the form of embrace or denial, or a bit of both.

The Matrix ignores both these paths; thematically, the film stages little or no polemic about pop culture. By setting itself after culture's end, it hasn't even the opportunity to display the problems of pop, much less to conceive of it as a kind of liberation from repressive authority. The closest the script comes is the occasional allusion: I suspect, for example, that Zion is named via *Neuromancer* more for Bob Marley's paradise than the biblical source (though the Zion rave in *Matrix: Reloaded* might send the most devoted populist, or rastafarian, heading for the ballet). Another example notable for its irrelevance to the plot[40] appears in the moment of Mouse's death: he goes out (presumably by his own choice, recalling that the Neb crewmembers have the capacity to load their own weapons and equipage into the Matrix) in a tragicomic replication of Tony Montana's fall at the climax of *Scarface* (this although the De Palma remake came out some 216 years earlier. Well, they're revolutionaries; they know their history.)

Such gestures are just that; they do not a position make. The film's cinematic form and social role make a different matter. From such a perspective, *The Matrix* is an extravagant celebration of its own status as a spectacle, and of its spectacular success. It could scarcely be further from the art-cinema austerity traditional to formal critiques of pop; its closest neighbour in the canon of philosophical sci-fi, *Blade Runner* (1992), seems closer in mood and measure to Bergman.

The special effects signal by themselves how ambitiously the film wants to be a bang-bang[41] crowd pleaser – how it believes such a condition to be the desirable form of moviedom, wrapped in surface pleasures so plentiful and substantial one might happily want for nothing more. Bullet time is merely the better half of the film's commitment to staggeringly expensive cheap thrills, even including related joyrides such as the full complement of combat sequences and the hyperdrop into loading programs used here and there (as when Morpheus and Neo descend to a rooftop or the desert floor). There are races against time, men quivering on ledges and a helicopter rescue climaxing in perhaps the most immaculate breaking of glass ever imaged: the vast building-face rippling liquidly on impact, hero swinging free just ahead of the geometrical shatter and ensuing fireball. Recounting that list, we can see why a director might say, 'It's about robots vs. kung fu' – not merely to palliate the inevitable claims of intellectual pretension, but because *The Matrix* contains everything that might be desired by a Saturday afternoon matineer.

Thrills and Bills

Commercial film is no more a set of cinematic than of economic performances. At the level of material truth, every scene is shot from the camera's point of view; by the same token, every piece of pop aesthetic must be seen from the point of view of money – not just in measuring its success, but in conceiving of what it communicates.

The Matrix was successful by any standards, including its own, which were unusually high: at the time, it was one of the more expensive films ever made. We may recollect it as a runaway success, a kind of majestic juggernaut. It's easy to forget it was far from being the year's cash king: it snuck narrowly into the top five, well behind *Austin Powers 2* and just a few grand in domestic receipts ahead of the animated *Tarzan*. And yet, as a cultural object it towers over its cohorts. Not only was it profligately influential on more than one tradition of film-making and on visual culture in general,[42] but it launched considerably more websites, discussion groups and late-night debates than *Tarzan*. And more than *Star Wars: Episode One*, which easily out-boxed its competitors.[43]

This may be definitive of the true products of pop culture: their cachet outraces their cashflow, if only by a second – a shockwave of fascination driven before an explosion of ten dollar bills. One buys not just a flip-down seat with a cup-holder, but a share of the object's success; this, in turn, becomes its own satisfaction (producing, eventually, contentless cult value, of which there are few better agents than the cartoon character Hello Kitty). One is joined with a vast and distributed crowd; the essential commonality is that everyone has chosen the same commodity.

Pop culture mystifies this neatly mercantile arrangement, promising that we can participate in the phenomenon rather than simply consume it. As such, it mirrors and is mimicked by the idea of the Matrix itself, a socioeconomic sphere expansively containing everybody, wherein passive audiences experience themselves as active players.

So is 'the Matrix' pop culture, then? Certainly this is an alluring solution. The title concept (and here we must credit Žižek) is so efficient at standing for various things, both abstract and concrete, that any simple answer to the question 'what is the Matrix?' will be at best both provisional and incomplete. 'Pop culture' is very much the kind of meta-answer required, capable of including a range of particulars as well as fluid concepts. It describes specific social and economic behaviours, and things one can touch and taste; it's also abstract enough to behave like the Matrix does, proliferating endlessly in our daily lives, shaping consciousness while seeming at times just a backdrop, at other times invisible. Nonetheless, it won't suffice. One evident drawback of such an answer is its elitism: the presumption that folks who mostly avoid pop culture are free of its – of the Matrix's – 'control'. Whether this is true or false as a description of our world,[44] it's a position extraordinarily at odds with the film's character. The Matrix scarcely promises we'll be rescued from mind-slavery by snobs.

The disjunction between the film's box-office success and cultural apotheosis starts to erode on closer inspection of the books. During its 25-week run in 1999, The Matrix earned something more than $171 million domestically. In wide (if uneven) overseas distribution, it grossed $258 million more. This is an unusual but not unheard-of breakdown; it's typical of Hollywood films that are not reliant on extensive or particularly nuanced dialogue. This chiefly includes action movies, and the potentially overlapping category of children's films (animated features are particularly easy to dub into foreign languages; Tarzan, for example, racked up remarkably similar numbers: $171 and $278 million, respectively).

Such an economic profile suggests the extent to which The Matrix succeeds in appealing to audiences with little or no commitment to it as a film of ideas. This doesn't imply that the reception beyond the initial market of the United States is thoughtless; just that the film stands on its own as a spectacular entertainment. We can be certain one of the elements of Hollywood film especially appealing to foreign audiences is American-ness – or some version thereof, as long as it's not hermetic Americana. If an action film can offer a lead endowed with internationalismo, so much the better.

Here Keanu Reeves's portable looks make for a distinct advantage (Speed, his other action hit, earned almost twice as much abroad as at home[45]). His passive, post-national beauty offers itself up to a broad spectrum of viewers. With his capacity to motivate desire, in combination with his lack of any affect or manner that might obstruct identification, he might be said to offer a visual analogue for Žižek's surmise regarding the philosophy of The Matrix: an alluring cipher wherein any audience might find both itself and its wishes. Or perhaps it would be simpler to say that Reeves's blank isn't white but silver; he has the most cinematic of faces. The blankness has its virtues beyond the silver screen as well: Reeves's peculiar availability is ideal for the viewer used to assuming the position of the videogame hero. This is a bodily leap more than a cathexis; most videogames, like most action heroes, ask more for a physical identification than emotional investment. By that token, *The Matrix* is structured as a game that toggles between so-called first-person and third-person shooters. Such flexibility, to move from a pseudo-objective view to point-of-view and back, was once the purview of films; videogames, for their early history, were one or the other.[46]

Pop pleasures (bottom left: *Scarface*, Universal Pictures, 1983)

Still, we should't discount the obvious in considering the extent to which *The Matrix* resembled a videogame (at least not within its initial moment; four years later it would, famously, *be* a full-featured videogame released concurrently with the first sequel, featuring film footage unavailable elsewhere). That it wanted the gamer audience is unmistakable, but the fissure between game and film is irredeemable. One can be played, and one cannot.

The Play's the Thing

Sort of. There's a mediating point, however inexact. The Digital Video Disc (DVD) gives the viewer at least a modicum of control over the film's

The most cinematic of faces (top: *Speed*, Twentieth Century Fox Film Corporation, 1994)

operation, using the remote control in a crude parallel of the gaming console with its controller. And one gets to do it at home.

At the beginning of 1999, the DVD market was in its infancy; it wasn't entirely clear how – or if – it would mature. The previous attempt at upgrading home-video media for the digital age, the laserdisc, had failed. The DVD had a variety of advantages, mostly coming down to a substantial increase in the ratio between data storage and physical size; like *Johnny Mnemonic*, it's a story of memory.

Billboard Magazine didn't bother to keep a DVD chart for 1998, coincidentally another bad year for Warner Bros. in the home market (in 1997, they had none of the five most successful home-video releases, and only one of the top thirteen; the next year was scarcely better). Nineteen ninety-nine was the first year DVDs merited a chart of their own. Market leader *Armageddon* had been available all year; *Titanic*, by some measures the most successful theatrical release in history, hit stores for home purchase in September. With such popular offerings (and, more importantly, a substantial increase in ownership of DVD players), the ground shifted as if at once. In the UK, for example, sales for 1998 totalled 180,000 units. In 1999, a single title sold 200,000 copies in December alone.

That title was *The Matrix*. In the USA, during its first week of release, it eclipsed the year's cumulative sales of *Armageddon*, and tripled those of *Titanic*, sending home 1.3 million discs (nearly $25 million). It topped the first-ever year-end chart without breaking a digital sweat; more impressive by far, it held its hegemony in the volatile popular market for 2000 as well. In both years, Time Warner was the leading home-video supplier in the land.

Successful in the theatre, it was a watershed in the home, essentially inventing a market. This sort of superpresence is far from being solely an economic fact. It chimes rather harmoniously with the script's conception of immanent image projection: like the Matrix, *The Matrix* is the movie that's everywhere, and was designed to be so.

It would be difficult to conceive of a film better designed to drive such a new market. There is a wealth of ancillary reasons: perplexing

details, clues and visual gestures aplenty to reward further viewings, if for no other reason than to confirm the narrative logic, enumerate the reflections in Morpheus's mirrorshades or notice the Mannerist wink of Parmigianino's *Self-Portrait in a Convex Mirror* in a convex door knob.

It seems likely, however, that the main attraction the film held for the home audience lay in the opportunity to review the virtuoso effects. If bullet time has a substantial displeasure, it's that it happens too quickly and slips away well before the sense of amazement. The DVD solves this problem neatly and absolutely, allowing one to return to the sequences at leisure – to *play* them. The power over the experience is limited, to be

Made to be frozen: micro-images for the DVD era

sure. Yet it is in several ways as close to gaming as it is to sitting in a theatre: We select a constructed world and its features, leap at will from scenario to scenario. And it's within our grasp to accelerate, slow or stop the action.

The film is scarcely unaware of its collapse of various territories of the pop image into a unified, expansive sphere that immerses the home viewer, the filmgoer and the gamer equally. One need only consider the jacket copy on the back of the original DVD release. It starts with a minimal précis. '**Perception**: Our day-in, day-out world is real. **Reality**: The world is a hoax, an elaborate deception spun by all-powerful machines of artificial intelligence that control us. Whoa.'[47] Summary out of the way, it unleashes a hail of discourse: 'Mind-warp stunts. Techno-slammin' visuals. Mega-kick action.' This simply isn't the language of film – even the most juvenescent B-movie reduced to the most telegraphic marketing come-ons. It's the language of videogames. The 'see-and-see-again cyberthriller' (thanks for the free advice) has not reached its newest, best form – it has exceeded its category.

With this, the circle of identifications (a great arc within the sphere of the commodity) draws close. The film does its best, stylistically and narratively, to replicate the immersivity of a videogame. It offers unimpeded physical identification with its heroes, computer workers who become action heroes immersed in a world of code that generates images. Their powers are those of the gamer, with exceptional fighting skills premised on a mastery over space and particularly over time. In turn, the DVD form offers the viewer a semblance of the gamer's active participation – a control sweetly congruent with the control acquired by the characters. The leads can freeze the scene and ponder what to do next, or accelerate out of real time; in the comfort of your own home, control in hand, so can you.

In the Realm of the Appearances

The Woman in Red sequence mentioned earlier (the DVD chapter listing refers to it as 'The Gatekeepers') plays out this drama generously. Neo's training doubles as our own; Morpheus soliloquises while leading Neo against the tide of a thronged city sidewalk that looks for all the world like the one across which Neo had earlier been dragged during his arrest. The elder rebel navigates the oncoming hurly-burly gracefully, as if he had seen it all before. Neo, conversely, finds himself stumbling into or awkwardly dodging the human traffic as he gawks (though his ease increases as the duo moves along). The crowd is an almost indistinct mass of black and white, mostly by way of business clothes, though the camera glances across at the occasional nun or sailor and even holds for a moment on the lone figure of a jackbooted police officer writing up a ticket. Well, these are business clothes too; the work status of the passersby is integral to Morpheus's explication, in which the only available roles are defined by labour.

The Matrix is a system, Neo. That system is our enemy. But when you're inside, you look around. What do you see. Business men, teachers, lawyers, carpenters. The very minds of the people we are trying to save. But until we do, these people are still a part of that system, and that makes them our enemy. You have to understand, most of these people are not ready to be unplugged. And many of them are so inert, so hopelessly dependent on the system that they will fight to protect it … Were you listening to me Neo, or were you looking at the woman in the red dress?

Viewer as king, with throne and sceptre

Neo, like any red-blooded, newly freed mindslave who had been living in a pod for some twenty-odd years, was looking indeed.[48] 'I was—,' he starts, before his instructor cuts him off: 'Look again.' Neo turns and we fly into his point of view just as a huge pistol speeds toward the camera, all but touching our eye. Behind it, Agent Smith; Neo ducks in panic. Morpheus methodically demands of the heavens: 'Freeze it.'

For the ten-thousandth time in film history, the cocking of a gun precedes the imperative 'freeze'; on this occasion it isn't the command of the gunplayer. The world freezes: the gun, Smith, the whole cityscape with its rushing mob. Though not actually a use of bullet-time technology, the scenario crystallises something about the *experience of bullet time* at its most refined. No wires, no flurries of fisticuffs or ammunition rain – just the rebels exercising their prerogative to exist out of Matrix time.

The first temptation (not for the first time) is to notice the metafilmic, the resemblance of Morpheus's demand to the director's 'Cut!' that shifts the world from sequence to pure *mise en scène*, commutes the extras to props and mannequins placed on a stage, among which the principals might wander, blocking out some drama for a future moment when it will count.

Sometimes, however, freeze means freeze. Morpheus isn't the man with the viewfinder but the man with the remote.

If we're to reside in the prefix anyway, it would be better to interpret this sequence not as metafilmic so much as metaspectational. The Matrix, and the various 'loading programs' within it, comprise a sphere of pure appearance, of the image as the total fact. 'The Gatekeepers' lays bare the most radical instance of this, the ultimate triumph of appearance over life: the visible decay of human into image. The human after all, the vivid subject, ought to be that thing least reducible to appearance (so, at least, goes the supposition of rational humanism).

We know the film is thematically suspicious (to say the least) of false images; what this sequence invites us to acknowledge is the extent to which absolute spectatorship is also a seductive sensation, if a little unsettling.

Passing strangers

The Finale of Seem

In the idea that the world is entirely at one's disposal, and that other humans are phenomena similarly disposed, lies a sense at heart that of omnipotence.[49] It's an apocalyptic omnipotence, or perhaps a mad one.[50] Rupert Pupkin, the aspiring comedian in *The King of Comedy* (1983), lines his room with a *trompe l'oeil* studio audience to laugh riotously at his routine, producing the illusion of his own triumph with a clunky array of consumer audio devices. In *The Quiet Earth* (1985), the last man alive (as far as he knows) stages a balcony address for a simulated host. It's not enough that they observe his imperial magnificence; they must celebrate it. This requires a sound system rigged with pre-recorded applause; a remote control plays its part.

In the kingdom of pure appearance. Right: *The Quiet Earth* (Capricorn Films International, 1982). Below right: *The King of Comedy* (Embassy International, 1982)

The part it plays is to secure the connection between the home viewer and the only human alive. It is in this circumstance that *The Matrix* inhabits itself most fully. In the movie house, we watch in groups as the celluloid unspools beyond our command. The DVD we watch alone, or perhaps with our select crew. And this, finally, is the sensation of the home viewer, reclining on the couch late in the night, the soundtrack drowning out any noises beyond the room. This had perhaps always been the secret emotional state of the home-movie enthusiast; now more than ever. The house is quiet and the world is calm. There is only the spectator, and the images fairly amenable to remote control. As with a videogame, played against a welter of computer-generated combatants, his is the only consciousness in the world.

Perhaps we would wish to wake from this, out of loneliness. But not just yet. There is a pleasure in being at play in the world of pure appearance, the world of things. It's like being alone in a total shopping arcade, armed with an unlimited budget (George Romero's 1978 film *Dawn of the Dead*, with prescient genius, sets the conflict between the last humans and the zombie hordes within a vast, echoing mall). It's consciousness as pure consumption: there are only objects, yours for the taking. No wonder bullet time debuted in television advertisements, in which the dance of commodities is stilled so that any might be easily grasped: its own logic wouldn't have it any other way. We can have anything – except the verb 'to have' seems to have stopped working. The images are just that. There are no things but in appearances, and having is limited to looking at them.

This is less the promise of the movie, as a viewed experience, than that in which it revels: the rhetoric of the social object called *The Matrix*. It is entirely spectacular. It swears that the only consciousness is that of the viewer, that ten-dollar demigod to whom all things offer themselves. If all movies bear the pleasure of spectatorship, *The Matrix* ferries it to the furthest shore, where spectating not only stands in for living but is the only form of life. And still it would be finally wrong to see that this world is composed of images. We might say instead that the world is composed of belief in them. The images are cast by the belief that there is nothing but images, nothing but that which appears.

5 Bad Spectacle

So long as the realm of necessity remains a social dream, dreaming will remain a social necessity. The Matrix is the bad dream of modern society in chains, expressing nothing more than its wish for sleep. The Matrix is the guardian of that sleep.

Thesis 21

A ruling class has achieved dominant power. There is a dominated class. The master class does not rule simply for the pleasures of power; neither may it simply destroy the underclass, as it requires something of them for its own sustenance: the physical energy naturally available in the human body, renewed every day until death. The ruling class's basic logistical issue: how to convince the underclass to offer up said energy, while at the same time keeping them alive but unresistant. The more of their energy that can be taken, and the less material that must be given in return, the greater the degree of domination – 'control', as Morpheus has it.

It's uncertain whether this even qualifies as allegory. If we call the master class 'the master class' rather than 'machines', and let the underclass keep that moniker, *The Matrix* is a plain-spoken Marxist description of capitalism and its human conditions. Nothing has been changed but the name – and that not by very much. Matrix, Marxist; what's a letter between friends?[51]

Society of the spectacles

The movie has clear antagonists with evident desires; the conflict of these desires drives the story. The subject of the combat – what everyone is fighting for – is the consciousness of the vast portion of the underclass, still unaware that they live cradle-to-grave[52] in chains, if it can be called living at all. A few representatives, having escaped their sub-lives of benumbed labour and having achieved consciousness of actual conditions, seek to awaken their unconscious sisters and brothers. The master class, in turn, must stop the underclass from realising that it's being mercilessly exploited, so as to maintain their provision of physical labour.[53] Something is keeping the human bodies enslaved; this something must be undone to free them.

This remains Marxism, of such textbook schematism that ignoring it starts to seem like wilful blindness, if not indeed bad faith. But this is not the *plot* of the movie; it's the circumstance of the world in which the story unfolds, and the engine of the narrative.

It may be the circumstance of our world as well. But, recalling the mandate to return always to particulars, to our historical moment, it's worth stating the obvious: the film was not made in 1848. History has not marched in quite the defile foreseen by Marx, who believed absolute crisis was inevitable, given the inequities between classes. After 150 years without seeing a world workers' revolution, the critical question of modern Marxism has become, in simplest form, why not? Modern thinkers, thus, focus considerable energies on how it is that the inequities remain tolerable or even invisible. The plot of the movie, like the plot of Marxism itself, turns on the question, 'What is the thing that stops the oppressed class as a whole from recognising its condition and immediately rising up?'

Or, as the film phrases the question, 'What is the Matrix?'

(Always Already) through the Looking Glass

The Matrix is not merely the technology of false appearance, but its illusion that each human consciousness is not utterly divided from the others – that there is a normal human sphere where people freely love, labor, go dancing, sleep and wake. The Matrix is not a collection of images; rather it is a social relationship between people that is mediated by images.

The kind of mediation that concerns us refers to the condition 'where certain social agencies are seen as deliberately interposed between reality and social consciousness, to prevent an understanding of reality'. This is from Raymond Williams's *Keywords*[54]; he is describing the negative use of term in the Marxist tradition, 'in a contrast between real and mediated relations, mediation being then one of the essential processes not only of consciousness but of IDEOLOGY'.

Ideology, in turn, involves the taking of social ideas for perpetual truths about the world, rather than as expressions of power relations in a particular society, place and historical moment. We accept as facts what are merely claims – claims that serve the master class in maintaining their control. Again, it's near impossible to describe these concepts without summoning quite directly the conceit of *The Matrix*.

Ideology is a glass through which we view the world, colouring what we see while at the same time endeavouring to be so well scrubbed that it itself disappears, leaving a seemingly clear view to what we are promised is The Real. In the words of the art historian T. J. Clark, 'Ideologies naturalize representation, one might say: they present constructed and disputable meanings as if they were hardly meanings at all, but, rather, forms inherent in the world out there.' He might as well be describing the scene that opens this book, in which Cypher stares at the screens filled with machine language and sees no code, no screen: 'You get used to it. I don't even see the code, all I see is blond, brunette, redhead. …' But then Clark might as well be describing the entire world of the Matrix in its grand flat expanse, and in a way he is: 'ideologies', he says elsewhere, 'are constructs'.[55]

If *ideology* describes the world of the Matrix, *The Matrix* describes the world of ideology. It does so with the pictorial grace and economy typical of the film's genius. The first scene of Neo at work (and within the film's political economy, the Matrix must orbit around work) is pointedly designed to illustrate what will be at play throughout the film, and without which the film cannot be understood. It's shot, brazenly enough, through a large plate-glass window, which just happens to be in the midst of being cleaned. Initially, our eye alights on the window, caught by the swash of soap and dirt. Two figures are dimly visible behind it. A polished squeegee swipe (a reminder also of that cinematic editing convention, the 'wipe') and the window approaches gleaming transparency; now we are looking through, at Neo and his corporate boss, Rhineheart.

This sequence is one of the film's multiple plays with the light on/light through binary – a distinction made for media, after all. As the window first becomes clear, Neo is staring almost directly at the theatre. Or is he glancing out at the panoramic view, at the window-washer, the camera, us? It's a look that betrays a pensive suspicion, as if he is starting, not to pierce the veil, but to see the veil, see mediation in action. Rhineheart, meanwhile, focuses on his monitor; on the wall behind them, a rectangle of Chicago skyline could be another window, or perhaps a mirror, or perhaps (so it finally seems) merely a framed picture. Why have a reproduction of the city that you see every minute out of your window? Perhaps it's as simple as the commonplace sigh of post-modernism, ruing how the fake has replaced the real. But this turns out to be another convenient yet false binary, proposing to explain things while excluding the crucial fact: there is no real here. Within the confines of the Matrix, there's no way to prefer one image to another, much less one *kind* of image to another; every single one is similarly falsified. Nothing is not mediated. Everything on which our gaze alights is an ambiguous screen through which, or on which (what could this distinction mean anymore, when the sun itself is a sham?), images are passing for the real.

And for us, looking on, the situation is not so different; even if the camera passes like a ghost through Rhineheart's window (as if that window were not hard but software), we see always through the camera lens (and by extension, through the arsenal of cinematic device) – the lens that is, just so, generally in the business of vanishing into a false transparency.

It all seems dizzying, an infinite regress for the viewer trying to understand the view. The film offers us some degree of steadiness, however. If we know enough to suffer the vertigo of spiralling irreality in the Matrix, with its collapsing image regime, it's because we're seeing the movie for the second time (a common urge, even if measured only by all those DVD sales). As a result, we know in turn that reality is secured for us, outside the Matrix: the *Neb*, Zion, the desert of the real. Just as in political philosophy, reality lies out there past ideology, beyond the construct.

In this opening scene, however, we are still moving inward, toward the centre of the Matrix, the heart of ideology; having established both the scene and the system of ideas by shooting through the plate glass, the point-of-view leaps into the room (pointedly looking back at the window-washers as a first bit of business).

So what do we encounter through the looking glass, within a sterile managerial office of the Matrix? What are the forms of this ideology, the forms that promise they're natural, inherent in the world in there?

You have a problem with authority, Mr Anderson. You believe that you are special, that somehow the rules do not apply to you. Obviously you are mistaken. This company is one of the top software companies in the world because every single employee understands that they are part of a whole. Thus if an employee has a problem, the company has a problem. The time has come to make a choice, Mr Anderson. Either you choose to be at your desk on time from this day forward or you choose to find yourself another job. Do I make myself clear?

Clear as a window.

The speech is all we'll know of Rhineheart, and all we need to know in this lifetime, though (or, rather, exactly *because*) it could be spoken by anyone in his position; it is the soliloquy of middle management. Inevitably, it presents an inescapable totality. Individuals are part of a whole; the whole is the company; 'the rules' (what rules?) apply equally to everyone and have no outside. Just so Rhineheart's offered choice between This Job and Some Other Job: a choice that presumed long ago that life is made totally of labour. A convenient belief for the proprietors of the Matrix.

The false binary that occupies all territory is indispensable for ideology; it banishes other conceptions from the realm of the thinkable. At best, they can creep in at the margins of consciousness, casting shadows that form the sentence, 'There must be something else.' Just so the Matrix: the achieved belief that its images are the real world in total form. The Matrix cannot be understood either as a deliberate distortion of the visual world or as a product of the technology of the mass dissemination of images. It is far better viewed as a *Weltanschauung* that has been actualised, translated into the material realm – a worldview translated into an objective force.

If some of us are shy about invoking such abstractions conversationally, *The Matrix* is not. While its speeches can't match the economy of the film's visual vocabulary, the Brothers have at least struggled to condense some of the more complex concepts of Western political theory into efficient theses. These in turn are pressed into double duty: plot points no less than philosophical musings. If the movie was titled *The Marxist*, Morpheus's pre-pharmaceutical speech to Neo would simply count as exposition:

MORPHEUS: What you know you can't explain. But you feel it. You've felt it your entire life. That there's something wrong with the world. You don't know what it is but it's there, like a splinter in your mind driving you mad. It is this feeling that has brought you to me. Do you know what I'm talking about?

NEO: The Matrix?

Mirror shades

MORPHEUS: Do you want to know what it is? The Matrix is everywhere. It is all around us, even now in this very room. You can see it when you look out your window or when you turn on your television. You can feel it when you go to work, when you go to church, when you pay your taxes. It is the world that has been pulled over your eyes to blind you from the truth.

NEO: What truth?

MORPHEUS: That you are a slave, Neo. Like everyone else you were born into bondage, born into a prison that you cannot smell or taste or touch. A prison for your mind.

Right – that's more or less the story, at least in its pre-revolutionary movement: ideology literalised.[56]

What's more, Morpheus seems determined that we don't miss out on the mechanics of the allegory. Window, television, 'world that has been pulled over your eyes' – what more could one want by way of cues? Nor do work, church and taxes seem like neutral choices; they're exactly what Louis Althusser refers to in describing how 'ideological state apparatuses' reproduce, in the incantatory phrase, the producers necessary for production. The Matrix makes labour. For all the robots and kung fu, all the videogame kicks, ideology is the plot.

Why Are These People Wearing Sunglasses?

Certainly the Matrix is ideology, but such a generality cannot finally be satisfying. Per ideology's own rules, mustn't there be a formulation of the Matrix particular to its place and time?

The mirrorshades know the answer. They're one of the film's obsessive details: a nod to cyberpunk tradition, plus they look cool. Each character has his own stylised shape, just as each character was assigned by Wo Ping a signature fighting move. At times they seem doubly comical: the ease with which they maintain precarious perches as bodies are hurled and battered about (especially in the case of Morpheus's stemless pair); and their tendency to be worn in rather sunless circumstances.

These oddities seem less strange when we notice that, by and large, the shades in question are worn only inside the Matrix. This would explain why our heroes, and their nemeses the Agents, have little difficulty keeping their eyewear balanced; they've transcended the physical laws that bind everyone else to the construct. Neo, for example, isn't allowed his own pair until he returns to the Matrix to rescue Morpheus. The lenses distinguish the people who know that the Matrix isn't the world but a mediated worldview, and have realised the power to change it; a sign of what was earlier termed 'superconsciousness', of mastery within the simulation.

They're certainly not optical devices; who would need such a thing in the Matrix, which is itself a huge optical device? Their very unnecessariness underscores the symbolic gesture: each set of lenses is a stylised version of the mediating screen that tints the world without itself appearing. The comedy remains, if in slightly different terms: the film's lead characters comprise a little society of the spectacles.

The Society of the Spectacle is a French book of political economy written by Guy Debord. In its most familiar English-language edition (a

'Like everyone else you were born into bondage …'

bootleg published by an anarchist collective; the author asserted no copyright), the cover showed a modified version of a photograph taken from the cover of *Life* magazine. Taken almost from the screen's point of view, it shows a movie audience staring ahead and slightly upward, engrossed in the feature; all wear 3-D glasses.

The book accepts the classic account of a social shift from a phase of *being* to a phase of *having*. Its significant extension is to describe a world that has entered a phase of *appearing*. In this society, spectacular images reign, and those with the power to produce them, to manage the symbols that seem to occupy the breadth of the public sphere, reign supreme.

This answers the question of how an underclass, floating in images, would be unable to see its sea of troubles and, by opposing, end them. The vast efforts of those in power go into disguising actual conditions, against any such revelation. History itself must be concealed under a welter of false appearance, lest it be recollected and awoken from. Thus, one quality of this period is that history has in effect disappeared. Time has stopped for everyone. If the machine of history must eventually drive toward revolution, the 'spectacle' serves to lock the machine's gears in place, while providing the appearance of forward motion.

This is as lovely a summary as we might find on offer: the Matrix is what stops history from happening. And so we return once more to bullet time, finally the film's signature not simply because of its visual ecstasy, but its aptitude – for the way it holds all the strands of the film together. The shadow-humans who know only the Matrix are not stopped in their tracks by bullet time, but simply revealed in their actual condition: frozen within unmoving time, trapped in the amber of the spectacle. Only our mirrorshaded heroes and villains, who know the world beyond the Matrix, are able to act, to exist in ongoing time as it rushes toward revolution (or is that *Revolutions*?); only they have awoken into living history. Bullet time, we might say, is the very opposite of a special effect. Just as its brief passages must seem to Neo or Trinity, these are moments of clarity for the viewer as well; bullet time shows the world as it is.

Within the Matrix, it's everything else that's a special effect. Because history itself is the spectre haunting modern society, pseudo-history has to be fabricated at every level of the consumption of life; otherwise the equilibrium of the *frozen time* that currently holds sway could not be preserved. The Matrix, being the reigning social organisation of a paralysed history, of a paralysed memory, of an abandonment of any history founded in historical time, is in effect a false consciousness of time.

The book fails as a summary of the world of *The Matrix* only insofar as it was published thirty-odd years before the film's release. And so one has little choice but to reverse the relation, to see the film as a rather expansive literalising of the book. In essence, it takes the conceptual world of *The Society of the Spectacle* to its abject endgame, where the underclasses labour twenty-four hours a day, and the spectacle disguising their condition is total. At certain points, the film seems intent on doing nothing more – or less – than quoting Debord's book in a filmic context, removing where necessary the word 'Spectacle' and inserting 'Matrix' in its place.

The Society of the Matrix

The phantasm that is the Matrix, as with the Woman in Red simulation, exists specially for each consciousness; in the nightmare of the real, each human is genuinely alone, isolated in a pod, pumped for its power (alas, to the machine-class each is indeed an 'it'). Each is purely alienated, converted into abstract labour. Yielding up its only asset – the corporeal body – and replenished with nothing but the barest subsistence, each human is Johnny Mnemonic fallen on the hardest of times, blinkered to what each is doing to earn its keep. They may think they're conscious and free, but each is having its own dream of life.

This grim truth casts its pall in the Matrix, wherein community is only a shadow play. Bodies may be in the same place, but nothing happens collectively; scene after scene is shot to emphasise the isolation of the individual. Green filtering creates a 'sickly' ambience (according to Bill Pope, the film's Director of Photography); the entire synthworld takes on a static, dead appearance that finds its apex in the fluorescent overheads of the Metacortex cubicle farm. This is only fitting; the optical manipulations of the lighting do the same work of separation as cubicle architecture itself.

These are the two main cinematographic strategies used for the synthworld, designed to alienate Neo from the others and to highlight that alienation. When Choi and company visit his solitary room, he insistently holds his position on one side of the doorway, set apart.[57] And when he follows them to the club, he remains distinct from the group; the focal depth underscores his separation.

It's here the rule demanding that Neo's body be divided from others is broken for the first time – by Trinity, fittingly, an emissary of the world beyond the Matrix. Here integration replaces alienation; the cell-like cubicle and garret give way to the crowded deck, grunge replaces sterility. Even the heroic rebels' little respites coded within the synthworld promise

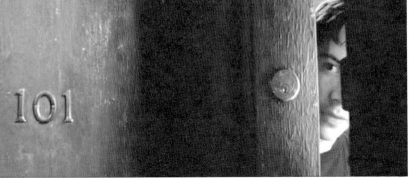

The loneliness of the tech worker

collective pleasures, from the overthrow of bad reality to the warmth of freshly baked cookies in the homey habitations of the Oracle.

The fact that these few, the rebels, are preponderantly women and/or people of colour is one of the political charms of the movie – particularly if we take Keanu's featureless feature-film features to signal Not a White Guy (though nothing can ameliorate the fact that he is the whitest and guy-est of the *Neb*'s crew, and, as it happens, the chosen one). It's heroic Marxism for the multicultural era; in that light, it's predictable enough that the other two white males in our rag-tag vanguard end up dead (Mouse) or as betrayers of the revolution (Cypher). It also lays bare the misfortune of the script's messianic strand, already such a dull invention compared to the film's conceptual nuances: the story of multicultural triumph can only end with the realisation of the collective – the many – where very different people have equal stake. Messianic narratives, like the most traditional Hollywood tales, concern the power of the individual hero – the one – even if the final act of heroism is self-sacrifice.

The Final Soliloquy of the Interior Paradox

This contradiction is small beer compared to the irreconcilable differences *The Matrix* has with itself, those tracked throughout this book: the film's delight in the power and pleasure of the new digital technologies against the dour cautionary tale of absolute danger at the end of the digital rainbow; in parallel, the story's far-reaching critique of the spectacular and the spectacle, so at odds with the movie's status as itself a spectacle. We'd like to suppose ourselves the liberated rebels fighting the power – but for the duration of the film, we can't help but resemble the docile labourers, each of us enclosed in our own chair, hooked to the popcorn and Coke machine, consuming digitised and mediated images that sing to us our own autonomy while returning our labour to the economy a few dollars at a time.

These aren't ironies but constituent contradictions; without them, the film's a trifle. *The Matrix* compels because within the complex of its story and its objective nature, its philosophy and economy, the film remains indeterminate, an unstable object. It may even be suggested that the film's lesser contradictions – logical paradoxes, rather than social irreconcilables – are a shadow cast on the narrative by the superstructure; the conceptual mindbenders, the sound and fury that so delighted Žižek's idiot, are neither remarkable nor banal. They are merely inevitable, symptoms of the larger irresolvability.

That the film rises or falls on uncertainty is something it knows well enough. Having achieved super-consciousness, ready to step forth from his phone booth and rocket into the skies, Neo is filled not with passionate certainty but its superlative lack: 'I don't know the future. I didn't come here to tell you how this is going to end. ...' This unknowability is exactly the measure of life beyond the Matrix; within its confines, despite the appearance of things going forward, the future is not just knowable but already known.

By now we are all post-modern enough to endure this, well versed in undecidability and uncertainty. Or maybe we have spent enough time introspecting on Zen koans to nod knowingly over the mechanism of the puzzler that exists only *not* to resolve, to keep the mind from coming to dull rest. This is the last temptation of abstraction.

And yet. There we go, leaving history behind when promised not to do so. Instead of turning in a gyre of irresolvability, and instead of taking uncertainty as its own satisfaction, might we return the contradictions to daily life? Might we suppose that the hypertrophied ambivalence is a crucial experience of history *circa* 1999, in America, in the world of coders and information workers and data temps, the world outside the movie, outside the theatre, but still inside something that seems like an endlessly self-replicating, territorialising construct, one rushing toward a fully managed totality, one filled with pleasures but one where real life grows ever more fugitive, ever more unreal? Might we suppose this feeling is about something?

6 The Dreamlife of the Boom

We know only a single science, the science of history.

Marx, The German Ideology

It's about work.

Or perhaps, fearing the brutalism of single-sentence summaries, one could say rather that the major currents flowing through *The Matrix* (digitech, spectacle, ideology, false totalities, Marxism and the entertainment business, to get started) empty into the ocean of work. Not just any kind of work, but as it appeared to the film's core audience in the spring of 1999, absolutely material, yet inseparable from its abstracted double. So, then: work and the economy. Here was the great construct that had come to be the world as it is, the irrationally exuberant boom that extended its sphere every hour, such that there was no way to get to its edge, and who would want to, really?

Substantially in fact and entirely in the public imagination, the tech boom was driven by California-based companies but globally distributed, much like the entertainment industry. For those in the right place at the right time – in the right *sector* – the boom made a lot of money on an accelerated schedule. The week after *Dark City* opened, the Dow-Jones industrial average, driven by tech stocks, first crossed 8,500; it burst the magical

10,000 barrier the week *The Matrix* hit theatres; by the release of *The Thirteenth Floor*, it had climbed more than 2,500 points.[58] Watching it ascend became itself a digital spectacle, the triumph of American post-industrialism, of the information economy. In that fifteen-month span, during which there was never a moment when some cinema wasn't showing an Edge of the Construct film, the Dow built *one quarter* of its entire value, the highest value in a century of existence. And that was that, more or less: by 14 March 2001, the index was again below 10,000, where it settled.

It would be foolish to suggest these movies were written about the economy, even if the President had been elected on a platform that swore this was the answer to every single question: 'It's the economy, stupid.' It is not so much a question of what called these movies into being, but of who. This asks us to think not just about the folk heroes of the boom, the 'internet millionaires' who got rich overnight on a kewl piece of code, an Initial Public Offering, abashedly balancing stock portfolios and Nintendo consoles. The vast majority of the moviegoing class were not masters of the new economy, floating above the action. Nor were they the excluded, who knew of the boom as little more than a fairytale, happening somewhere else, in the vapour, to people one would never meet. They were the bio-power of America's very own bubble economy, where for a few dozen months no one deigned to distinguish between solid capital and the endlessly proliferating imaginary cash created by a consensual hallucination. What had seemed like fixed economic laws were temporarily suspended (have I mentioned bullet time?). Productless companies rocketed shareholder value into the dreamosphere, because everyone believed. In Silicon Valley, people were buying real McMansions they didn't have time to furnish, with fictional money from stock options that couldn't be cashed in just then. Virtual money. Matrix money.

The Matrix isn't just a totem of the era, but its ultimate product: a massively capitalised, wickedly digitised convergence of industry and desire. When the go-go tech workers of 1999 drank up *The Matrix* in their few moments of downtime, they were consuming their own ecstatic achievements. Hollywood, especially in its epic mode, sings to the audience the story of their waking lives moved to the faraway-near of allegory, where they might take on the drama that defines their quotidian experience through its very absence. This is a truism of genre fiction – and, no less, of the digital imaginary where a kid at his computer is 'Captain Crunch' or 'CGI Joe'. It is also the nature of the spectacle, promising that frozen lives are filled with intensity. Just so, a data temp imagines himself a coder; a coder imagines himself a hacker. A hacker imagines himself a rebel fighter, a console gamer an actual martial artist, and so on. In these fantasies of power and autonomy, the quotidian becomes the heroic; just as crucially, the digital becomes the material, the simulation converts to the real. *The Matrix* tracks these fantasies with poetic attention. It's the dreamlife of the boom.

The rest of the time, the film's audience, when they weren't an audience, laboured more than ever. The new economy had shrugged off the eight-hour day like an old husk. The border between work and not-work went with it. The phrases 'go to work' and 'go home' threatened archaicism. If the iconic image of the time was the programmer coding for 26 hours and nodding under the workstation, its flip side was the itinerant data temp, hustling a week here and a project there, wherever some start-up needed an IPO crash crew. The shock troops worked at a dozen cubicles in a month, at home, at the café next to the microbrewery; they had mobile phones and laptops but no medical insurance or weekends. In the words of an industry analyst, written in 1999, 'There aren't enough hours in the day or enough smart people in the world to do what we have – and want – to do.'[59] No place was beyond work; in effect, the hive of cubicles extended to every horizon. Even after the bust, the iconography of paradise was irrevocably infected. In 2003, a brochure for the Learning Annex (a loose-knit savoir faire centre – the first offer in this brochure is the 'Money Magic Get Rich Workshop') featured on its cover the enjoinder 'Make money on eBay. Even on vacation!' A bikini-clad woman reclines in a beach chair, her toes in the sand, cannily meeting the gaze of her laptop computer, apparently unvexed by the historical definition of the word *vacation*.[60]

Only one *fin de siècle* back, technology's singular vow was to make us all ladies and gentlemen of leisure. It was going to work for us. Now, in every place and at all hours, we worked for it. Except we didn't; it wasn't 'the machines' doing this to us; this is why the tracking of the man vs. machine cliché is a dead end. Technology just made it all more convenient. These were halcyon days for the empire of work, in its colonisation of everyday life.

This is the dystopia on offer in *The Matrix*.

Mergers and Acquisitions

The concept of 'the Matrix' might stand for 'ideology' or 'the spectacle' – might in fact be indistinguishable from them. But we ought not look too far into the ether and lose sight of our own noses. The Matrix resembles more concretely the endgame of millennial merger mania – what happens when all the corporations of the world become one seamless super-entity within which you labour, eat, make love, pay rent (*The Truman Show* offered a different version of the same surmise, openly fingering the entertainment-industrial complex and thus offering a less expansive but more efficiently self-cancelling object).

The Matrix cannot be abstracted from this processional. Warner Bros., a not particularly volatile Hollywood fixture, had wed similarly venerable Time Inc. in 1989; during the 1990s, the new entity ate like an adolescent and mated as if in heat. By 1995, Time Warner was the world's largest music publisher and had started its own television network; after 1996's landmark Telecommunications Act (an invitation to vertically integrated monopoly), it bedded Turner Broadcasting (the dowry this time including CNN, as well as a sundry other cable channels, film studios and professional sports franchises). It's here, in this period, that *The Matrix* goes into production, that all the Edge of the Construct films are released. By 2001, in the waning, nerve-burnt days of the boom, Time Warner would find itself in the marriage bed of history's largest merger. The great consummation was with a tech company, of course: America Online, the corporation that delivered the concept of an online community out of its gestation in the computer-geek subculture and into the world.

Such gargantuism was, in 1999, the order of the day. We can recognise how it's thrilling, as conquest is thrilling to watch, to take part in, even to be a subject of. We can see also the anxiety of being engulfed.

This is an ambivalent moment, in which the construct appears in all its glory on the verge of ceasing to be construct at all, just the world as it is. The evolution from Warner Bros. to AOL Time Warner required only a few years of corporate copulation. From AOL Time Warner to the Matrix – it's just a kiss away.

The transition already had its imaginary, in the irreplaceable source text of *Neuromancer*. Real life has not yet been overthrown, but already the villainous combine is a limitless and mystifyingly diversified corporate family, Tessier-Ashpool SA, overseen by a succession of clones, operated and protected by an Artificial Intelligence that has extended itself throughout space both cyber- and material:

The corporate code: there is no outside anymore

Power ... meant corporate power. The zaibatsus, the multinationals that shaped the course of human history, had transcended old barriers. Viewed as organisms, they had attained a kind of immortality. You couldn't kill a zaibatsu by assassinating a dozen key executives; there were others waiting to step up the ladder, assume the vacated position, access the vast banks of corporate memory. But Tessier-Ashpool wasn't like that, and he sensed the difference in the death of its founder. T-A was an atavism, a clan.

It is this last distinction that struggles to maintain sci-fi's failing wager that the present can still, at this late date, be defended against the post-human future – that, in *Neuromancer*'s terms, the invidious megacorp might still be stopped through some version of knightly combat. But such optimism finally fails; Tessier-Ashpool's AI escapes the climactic carnage and, a page from the end, reappears to the protagonist. 'So what are you,' Case wonders. Formerly known as Wintermute, the AI no longer has any need for a name: 'I'm the matrix.' If *Neuromancer*'s atavistic clan can be slain, the corporation they devised, with its implacable systemic superpresence, no longer offers anything with which the knight might tilt. Not even a windmill. This is no less true of AOL Time Warner than of Tessier-Ashpool or the Matrix.

This is perhaps why the heroic messianism of *The Matrix* seems so contrived, so dismissible. Such heroic fulfilments are exactly what we would expect from spectacle: the sort of fantasy that the Matrix's masters would program. Oughtn't a film so smart about the nature of the spectacle and 'control' have a better version of resistance? But then, perhaps a film without such a promise would be too bleak – too bleak, we trust, to recoup its expenses. Time Warner had, in a way, bet the lot on *The Matrix* – at least, for the first time, the opening image of the Warner's lot rippled past behind a Matrix-y scrim of phosphor green. The branding image used to be a last promise of the real before the celluloid dream began: *Here's the actual place where movies are made*. Even the premiere audiences for *The Matrix* had seen the previews and posters, knew what the colour signified: *There are no places any more. Just code.*

The Birth of Allegory

If *The Matrix* is the great allegory of the boom, its mirror is the rather modest comedy *Office Space* (1999), written and directed by Mike Judge, purveyor of the animated MTV serial *Beavis & Butthead*. It's not a remarkably comical comedy; its caper subplot is even more negligible. Nonetheless, unerring in its processed landscapes and corporate culturespeak, it's a Rosetta stone of the banalities pooling in the technology parks of Silicon Valley.

The narrative pits software engineer Peter Gibbons, and co-workers Samir and Michael, against their life of vacant and ever-expanding labour for a tech company. *Office Space*'s DVD packaging refers to its lead as 'cubicle slave Peter Gibbons'; the theatrical trailer offers 'a movie about

Welcome to the technology park of the real (*Office Space*, Twentieth Century Fox Film Corporation / 3 Arts Entertainment / Cubicle, 1999)

The heart of the construct

people who go to work ... and need to escape'. This alone ought be enough to put us in mind of *The Matrix* – the difference rests largely in whether the language of 'cubicle slave' is used figuratively or not.

There's more to recommend *Office Space* than its value as an analogy, and elements that exceed the tale of millennial wage-slavery. This includes, for example, the satisfying if politically incoherent episode in which the plot's three conspirators vent their frustration on the reviled office fax machine; the punishment, set to a gangster-rap soundtrack and meted out via baseball bat and stylised kicks, again recapitulates the beating of Rodney King.

The movie, that is, has room for other nightmares. But they do not career toward the riotous apocalypse threatened by *Strange Days*' millennium. The movie refuses to leap into allegory, or even hyperbole. The nightmare to which it always returns is the blunt quotidian of work; a nightmare as discomfiting for its ennui as its ensnarements. On the Friday of the plot's turning point, Peter attempts to dodge his blandly soulless boss Lumbergh amid the identical cubicle enclosures of Initech – but, like Thomas Anderson fleeing Agent Smith through the fluorescent abyss of Metacortex, it's to no avail.

Because this is no allegory, our hero isn't eluding the sinister representatives of a shadow regime – just the murmuring blackmail that is the natural language of the middle manager. Anti-heroic to its core (in reaction, one suspects, to the hero narratives endemic to the boom's self-mythologising), *Office Space* is 'the Matrix' portion of *The Matrix* with every trace of the uncanny evacuated.

No fantastical plane leaks into the real world. This defines the film; its world is one in which the imaginary has been utterly disallowed. Instead it tells the story of work as the ever-expanding construct in its most abject form. Caught by Lumbergh, Peter is subject to that increasingly familiar demand:

I'm gonna need you to go ahead and come in tomorrow. So if you could be here around nine, that would be *great*, mmmkay? Oh ... oh ... and I almost forgot: Ahh, I'm also gonna need you to go ahead and also come in on Sunday, too, mmmkay?

In the stylised *Matrix*, the cut-on-capture is to a classically uncanny interrogation (in which, we recall, the hero is shortly reminded of his destiny as pure labour: 'You're Thomas A. Anderson, program writer for a respectable software company, you have a social security number, you pay your taxes'). *Office Space* splices immediately to Peter's visit with an 'Occupational Hypnotherapist', for whom he limns, in his decent, crushed tone, the conditions of his working life:

I was sitting in my cubicle today and I realised ever since I started working, um, every single day of my life has been worse than the day before it. So that means that every single day that you see me – that's on the worst day of my life.

The soliloquy of the alienated worker is followed by the film's one reach toward a dreamworld, what we could call the originary fantasy that begets the bifurcated world of Thomas Anderson and Neo:

Is there any way that you could, sorta, just zonk me out so that, like, I don't know that I'm at work – in here [*pointing at his head*] – could I come home and think that I'd been fishing all day, or something?

There is no awakening from his nightmare, and the film knows it; the only escape from pure work is in the plea for a better dream. As if in answer, *The Matrix* would be released six weeks later.

Home Office

No wonder the multi-stage final battle of *The Matrix*, wherein Trinity and the now-superconscious Neo jack back into the Matrix to rescue Morpheus, must begin with a return to office architecture, to the dully grand corporate tower rising into a skyline built of nothing but business.

However, this is wish fulfilment of a scale only Hollywood could manage; such a move toward resolution expresses the film's theoretical problem all too well. Its 2199 allegorises the condition of the labouring classes at the end of our 20th century. But within the film's logic, its 1999 is the Matrix, the delusion, the acme of all ideology. The office building can't be destroyed; like Metacortex, it is itself an allegory, a tolerable symbolic expression of its 2199 real. For all its stark lines and modern appurtenances, its whirr of data in mid-process, it too is an archaism, two centuries behind

the times. In the desert of the real, the architecture has reached its apotheosis, not as frozen music but frozen life. The work-week is 168 hours; the cubicle has been reduced to a pod the worker need never leave – may never leave – where rudimentary needs are accounted for with maximum efficiency, immersion is total, and payment is delivered in appearance value.

The nightmare haunting *The Matrix* is that 1999's expanding construct – the working week and the workstation, the economy, the corporate sphere – can't be stormed at all. Architecture can only stand in its place. It's a mass of systems, agreements, leverages and interlocked interests of a complexity no individual can encompass, codified by documents no one sees. It's not a place, really, just a set of codes …

Thus the Matrix, that set of codes that has flowered into totality. It is not something *added* to the real world – not a decorative element, so to speak. On the contrary, it is the very heart of society's real unreality, capable of infinitely executing itself, and endlessly dissimulating the absence of the real. How then do we come to its edge?

It's not clear that we do. That is, there's no walking out of the Matrix, out of Truman's false town or Murdoch's Dark City, no stairway departing the Thirteenth Floor. There is the fundamental act of recognising that this is not the world as it is. This is easier said than done, and *The Matrix* knows it. On the deck of the rebel craft, when Neo first catches sight of the Matrix code, light through screens, the more

experienced (and corrupted) rebel Cypher is blind again: 'I don't even see the code.' What sounds at first as a deep gracefulness with the mechanics of reality is instead a wilful return to the nightmare; no wonder he manages to look like he's labouring, isolated, at yet another workstation.

We save a spoonful of sympathy for Cypher: he wants it back, the sensual world of *stuff*. He requires only basic things: 'I don't want to remember nothing. Nothing. You understand? And I want to be rich.' There is a pleasure in just sliding back into it, out of the shuddering ambivalence, letting the edge of it fade from view, letting the rain be nothing more than rain, not some green system raining down.

Notes

1 Though David Cronenberg's *eXistenZ* (1999) seems an obvious candidate for inclusion in this millennial deluge of virtual reality films, I would argue that it doesn't quite fit the specificities of the category. Its conclusion is ambiguous, but either the protagonists know accurately at the outset what reality is, or else the narrative is an infinite regress – a story in which every chapter ends 'and then I woke up'. In any case, the movie doesn't feature a pivotal moment when the heroes suddenly view the limit of what they had always thought was reality. However, *eXistenZ* – an extension of Cronenberg's longstanding fascination with video as social control – is plenty concerned with the increasing appeal of immersive videogaming, a topic that will return with a vengeance in Chapter 2.

2 Another reading of this movie, which opened on 5 June 1998, is that – for the audience – it was a form of mourning for one of the longest-running and most popular television shows in history: *Seinfeld* had aired for the last time twenty-two days earlier.

3 Recalling that, in his role as a tech worker within the Matrix, Neo is named Thomas Anderson, we can't help but wonder: why, exactly, all the extraordinarily WASPy names? It's as if the falsely normal worlds of the simulations require names of exaggerated normalcy. Or perhaps these are simply slave names, and they will all be free to choose their own liberonyms once they reach reality.

4 These commonplaces appear independent of sci-fi: the latter in Plato, for example, and the former in parables of the Industrial Revolution such as 'John Henry'. It might be said that the genre finds its rightful subjects in these pre-existent concepts, though it's more accurate to suggest that

sci-fi turns out to be a convenient holding cell for such anxieties.

5 The anarchist website Infoshop (www.infoshop.org), despite a general resistance to corporate products and slogans, periodically includes underneath its own title the admonition 'Take the red pill.'

6 *Total Recall* (1990) offers perhaps the textbook case in Dickian films, though the more ambiguous *Blade Runner* (1982) is a far more engaging film. Similarly, Dick provided the story for *Screamers* (1995), a classic bit of man vs. intelligent machine pulp, but again, this is a topic handled with far more subtlety in *Blade Runner*, which stands with *The Matrix* as a kind of sci-fi Alexandria. We've got it covered: see Scott Bukatman's *Blade Runner*.

7 From which the Gnostic worldview can be separated only through a religious commitment to the 'analytic' nature of philosophy. Descartes, in an early formulation, posited a malicious demon bent on falsifying the entirety of the perceived world.

8 Online chat 11 June 1999, archived at http://whatisthematrix.warnerbros.com/

9 And not just sci-fi – see, for example, the post-philosophy lecture discussion in *National Lampoon's Animal House*. More formally, the structure organises such disparate tales as Italo Calvino's novel *If on a Winter's Night a Traveller ...*, the Richard Linklater animated film *Waking Life* (2001), and Michael Jackson's 'Thriller' video.

10 When we first encounter Neo, he's behind a door numbered 101, which manages both to be binary code and promise his One-ness. A movie of signs and portents indeed.

11 If not long before. As the film scholar Louis-Georges Schwartz has argued, in the context of Hollywood films, it's actually rather hard to conceive of the director's artistic vision as such, and that we would do better to assume that any given movie is 'directed by money'.

12 It was this particular use, previewed in *The Matrix* trailer, that seemed to give the nascent effect (otherwise known to the film's tech guru John Gaeta as 'Flo-Mo') its adult name. Historians of the effect trace the title back a bit further, to the aforementioned Smirnoff's spot 'Smarienbad', by short form genius Michel Gondry, which also features a stilled bullet.)

13 Gibson has repeatedly denied responsibility for the genre, much like a deadbeat Gargantua anxious to avoid a life of responsibility for Pantagruel.

14 It seems important not to invest too heavily in exploring the full portfolio of the film's influences, what with everyone fighting so fiercely for a share. A leap into the fray lands inevitably on a slippery slope, where the Japanese anime contingent clashes with proponents of the underground comic *The Invisibles* and so on, in sort of shadow play reprising the disputes between theologians and philosophers. Or perhaps a reversed perspective is more accurate, and abstract debates are the shadows cast by popular culture.

15 The adaptation of *Neuromancer* is something like the Holy Grail to a generation of Hollywood knights; it's generally agreed that a film version would beggar the concept of 'a budget'. We can only hope that some noble Gancelot will someday marshal the chutzpah, backing and formal vision to screen its intricacies.

16 'Mirrorshades' occupy the acme of cyberpunk iconography, and provide a title to its canonical anthology, edited by Bruce Sterling (1988). The social history of these sunglasses remains to be written.

17 This structure would be recapitulated in 2003 by the film *Paycheck* (finally, some truth in titling), wherein Ben Affleck plays an engineering genius hired by companies to design tech commodities so valuable that his memory must be wiped upon completion, leaving him with lost time and a lump sum. Though far from the only film driven by anxieties about intellectual property rights, this particular telling marshals three charms: it phrases the issue overtly in terms of alienated labour, in the Marxist sense; it's based on a story by Philip K. Dick, securing further the Gibson/Dick genealogy; and it's a fine recounting of the Hollywood star's conundrum, between taking the single fee for a role, or sharing in the contingent profits.

18 There are a number of actors for whom inhabiting a traditional, naturalistic character is not really in the repertoire; they can't quite play human. And so they realise their talents through this very limitation, in the roles of characters not human but trying to pass. In this club, the Terminator vies with Daryl Hannah's mermaid in *Splash* (1984); Lance Henriksen's tender cyborg from *Aliens* (1986) encounters Kyle MacLachlan in his single great performance, as a human body under alien influence in *The Hidden* (1987).

19 We might argue, moreover, that Moss's pointed resemblance to Reeves makes her a convenient site of displacement for the hetero male audience, unready to fix on Keanu as their object of desire. Neo's initial exchange with Trinity is a wonder of economy in the codes of sublimated homoeroticism: 'I just thought, um, you were a guy,' he says fumblingly. Her comeback: 'Most guys do.' Imagine the relief of every straight guy in the room.

20 Though it's scarcely unheard of for new visual effects, particularly if they are cost-intensive, to be devised within commercial contexts, it nonetheless remains far more common for mainstream film to recuperate experimental devices than vice versa. An obvious example is Godard's jump-cut, now such a staple of the cineplex that its use is often ascribed to the pernicious influence of MTV-style editing, rather than the no-less-pernicious French. And even French art cinema draws on techniques from more experimental sources: consider the hand-modified filmstock of Olivier Assayas's *Irma Vep* (1996), echoing Stan Brakhage. Oliver Stone's *Natural Born Killers* (1994) is a veritable cinematic Tourette's Syndrome of avant-gardist exclamations.

21 For the dot-commer, the videogame in fact resembled work almost exactly, except it was fun and there was no boss.

22 Videogame-driven films were scarcely a late 1990s invention: witness *Tron* (1982) and *Super Mario Brothers* (1993). Previously, however, these seemed part of a general policy of cashing in on pop-cultural fads – of a piece with skateboarding movies or *Spice World* (1997). The competition heats up around 1995 with *Mortal Kombat*; by the watershed year of 2001, one could scarcely go to the cineplex without running aground on *Final Fantasy*, *Resident Evil* or *Lara Croft Tomb Raider*.

23 This is true even if we haven't, like Neo, Trinity, Morpheus and every fourteen-year-old in Indiana, acquired the 'cheat codes'. Because the action is responsive purely to the movements of the player, the single-player videogame is inseparable from the experience of being the point from which time flows.

24 That is, the one who most resembles the popular conception of the home gamer.

25 The Matrix, or, The Two Sides of Perversion', from 'Inside the Matrix' International Symposium at the Center for Art and Media, Karlsruhe, 1999.

26 Žižek stops short of an interesting idea: that this capacity, literally, is universally true of film, and is what separates it from theatre. In the latter, we might look out at the audience as an aggregate, or make eye contact with one among many. In the former, we need only lock glares with the lens to meet every gaze.

27 And which he indeed does directly, tarrying only one sentence: 'What, then, is the Matrix? Simply what Jacques Lacan called 'big Other,' the virtual symbolic order, the network that structures reality for us.'

28 The penultimate sequence of *The Matrix Reloaded* suggests Žižek's on the right track. Generally herein, I have endeavoured to ignore the two sequels, *Reloaded* and *Revolutions* (both 2003), in trying to understand *The Matrix* – not because they suck, but because the goal is to understand the first film's relationship to a particular moment in history, including its reception in that moment.

29 A shot of tequila every time Neo 'wakes up' in *The Matrix* would make for a fun, if potentially injurious, drinking game.

30 In 2003, when I asked Keanu Reeves what homework the Brothers assigned him for the new instalment, he said, 'They told me I could look at Schopenhauer and Hume and their old pal Nietzsche.' Reading Schopenhauer's *The World as Will and Representation*, he felt compelled to return to Hegel, and then to Kant, until, he conceded,

'I'm, like, dunno, I have to do some stretching and some kicking.'

31 The phrase will also be taken, in 2002, as the title for a brief volume by Slavoj Žižek. The monograph was one of three commissioned by Verso Press; the other two were by Paul Virilio and Jean Baudrillard.

32 A world the film invites you to imagine, no less fantastical than one in which *The Matrix* is 'about robots vs. kung fu'.

33 Whose debut had been the extraordinary *Near Dark* (1987), a bloody reinvention of the bloodsucker genre as AIDS allegory that stands with the best films of the 1980s.

34 The minidisc, a technology that never caught on in the United States, is Hollywood's default image for human memory storage in the digital age; in *Johnny Mnemonic*, Keanu's payload is uploaded from same. The *locus classicus* of human memory storage, Douglas Trumbull's *Brainstorm* (1983), imagined a far bulkier device, appropriate to the pre-digital era of tape drives *et al*.

35 Within the context of a Rodney King allegory, it's apparent why the dream of a video recording so total it might function as perfect, incontrovertible evidence is particularly appealing. However, the implicit idea that fallible evidence was responsible for the verdict in the officers' trial is a notable misunderstanding of technology's role.

36 What's an *r* between friends? Very little, but still more than an *s*, as we shall see in Chapter 5.

37 For yet another confrontation of this difficulty, see Wim Wenders's *Until the End of the World* (1991), preferably the director's cut. The film concerns the quest for a technology to allow the recording of experience for later playback; this somehow precipitates a reality crisis so profound that the film is set not against the Millennium, which is apocalyptic only in the figurative sense, but against apocalypse itself.

38 As it happens, the city replicated in *The Truman Show* is a classic sim-city: Seaside, Florida, a town designed and maintained by the Disney Corporation.

39 As Baudrillard himself notes, these thoughts on Disneyland are indebted to earlier works, two in particular. The semiotician Louis Marin had already meditated on Disneyland's symbolic structure, in *Utopiques, jeux d'espaces*. The systematic analysis of Michel Foucault is invaluable here as well, specifically his profound recognition about prisons: that they formalise the carceral relation so that the rest of us, on the outside, can cozen the belief that we are truly free.

40 The higher a percentage of a film's details attend to narrative or expositional necessity – we might call them *plotemes* – the more glaring the gestures that play no such part (which we might in turn call *spuremes*, after their spurious nature). A film with a high ratio might be thought of as functionalist; as the calculation decreases, we edge toward the baroque. In this regard, *The Matrix* is a highly functionalist film, and obviously proud of it.

41 Less so kiss-kiss.

42 A headline from *The Onion*, simultaneously parodying and indexing this influence: 'Bowling-Alley Owner Wants TV Ad To Look 'More Matrix-y'' (Vol. 39, Issue 25.)

43 *The Sixth Sense* and *Toy Story 2* round out the top five, meaning that three of the four films that outdrew *The Matrix* were sequels.

44 It is false.

45 Whereas dialogue-heavy *My Own Private Idaho* was considered all-but-unreleasable west of California and east of London.

46 This has changed noticeably in the years since 1999; many combat (and other) games now offer the player the option of shifting between views.

47 This trope, the Perception/Reality formula, is explicitly the language of political revelation. That's another story – or another chapter.

48 As Reggie Hammond (Eddie Murphy) says in *48 Hours* (1983), 'I've been in prison for three years. My dick gets hard after the wind blows.'

49 The erotics of this omnipotence are exactly what's at stake when Mouse offers Neo some time alone with the Woman in Red.

50 The supreme pre-cinematic case is probably that of Freud's patient Schreber, who in many regards might be considered the ideal audience for *The Matrix,* insofar as its world is his delusion made real.

51 Or perhaps we are to think of MATRIX as MARX + IT. What's IT again? Oh yeah: Information Technology.

52 Indeed, cradle, grave and work space are one; the elimination of time once lost commuting would surely bring glee to a Taylorist efficiency expert.

53 This is not the first time that sci-fi cinema has substituted genre villains for an economic class. To choose just one example, John Carpenter's *They Live!* (1988) imagines that the yuppies and overlords of its minimally futurised Los Angeles (where Bunker Hill has become so stratified along class lines that there is only the supergentrified heights and the shantytown below) are actually aliens. Armed with – what else? – special sunglasses, the hero Nada sees their real messages concealed within various media: televisions and billboards

proposing an endless programme of ideological control. *Stay Asleep. No Imagination. Submit to Authority.*

54 Raymond Williams, *Keywords* (New York: Oxford University Press), 1983, p. 206.

55 T. J. Clark, *The Painting of Modern Life* (Princeton: Princeton University Press), 1999, p. 8.

56 The narrative of ideological terror and the fantasy of being the last man alive are not strangers to each other. Indeed, the fantasy that one is the last free consciousness, as yet untainted by ideology, called to superhuman vigilance lest one be overtaken, has already been screened – it's called *Invasion of the Body Snatchers.* It's been made three times already: in 1956, 1978 and 1993. We might say it is America's national story, the one it remakes in times of crisis – akin to the Japanese film community's habit of refilming the story of the forty-seven ronin cyclically, most famously in Mifune's *Chushingura* (1962).

57 This kind of insistent architectural separation recalls the almost unbroken Renaissance tradition of Annunciation paintings, depicting the Virgin Mary divided from Gabriel by a wall, lintel, a window frame or some more curious structural invention. And, in its way, this scene functions in part as an annunciation: 'You're my saviour, man,' etc. However, it's scarcely the only episode of such architectural isolation in the film.

58 http://www.djindexes.com/jsp/avgStatistics.jsp#no3.

59 Kevin Bachus, *Maximum PC*, 1 August 1999.

60 Learning Annex brochure, November/December 2003.

Credits

The Matrix

USA/Australia
1999

Directed by
The Wachowski Brothers
Produced by
Joel Silver
Written by
The Wachowski Brothers
Director of Photography
Bill Pope
Editor
Zach Staenberg
Production Designer
Owen Paterson
**Music Composed,
Orchestrated & Conducted
by**
Don Davis

©Warner Bros.
(US, Canada, Bahamas &
Bermuda)
©Village Roadshow Films
(BVI) Limited
(All other territories)
Production Companies
A Warner Bros. presentation in
association with Village
Roadshow Pictures -
Groucho II Film Partnership
A Silver Pictures production
Executive Producers
Barrie M. Osborne
Andrew Mason
Andy Wachowski
Larry Wachowski
Erwin Stoff
Bruce Berman
Co-producer
Dan Cracchiolo
Associate Producers
Richard Mirisch
Carol Hughes
Production Accountant
Marge Rowland
**Production Accountant–
Australia**
Alistair Jenkins

1st Assistant Accountant
Mandy Butler
Assistant Accountant
Michele D'Arcey
Production Co-ordinators
Megan Worthy
2nd Unit:
Jane Griffin
Julia Peters
**Assistant Production
Co-ordinator**
Katherine Gamble
Unit Production Manager
Carol Hughes
Unit Managers
Will Matthews
2nd Unit:
Simon Lucas
Assistant Unit Managers
Grayden Le Breton
2nd Unit:
Dick Beckett
Locations Managers
Peter Lawless
2nd Unit:
Robin Clifton
Production Secretaries
Justine Vollmer
2nd Unit:
Lizzie Eves
Production Aides
Nathan Anderson
Sassica Donohoo
Marcus Dwyer
Juan Goldsmith
Marvin Hayes
Melissa Johnston
Alex Kaufman
2nd Unit:
Belinda Dean
Staff Assistants
Peter Forbes
Jayne Johnson
Tommy O'Reilly
Danielle Osborne
Janet Seppelt
Bryce Tibbey
Chris Whittle
Sinclair Whalley
Charly Wrencher
Luke Wrencher

Mark Fletcher
Michael Roth
Suzanne Middleton
Jane Healy
Sally Sharp
Donna Huddleston
Bianca Havas
Lea Lennon
Fiona Landreth
Belinda Lowson
**Assistant to the Wachowski
Brothers**
Phil Oosterhouse
Assistant to Joel Silver
Michelle Tuella
**Assistants to
Barrie M. Osborne**
Annie Gilhooly
Angela Pritchard
Assistant to Andrew Mason
Emma Jacobs
**Assistant to
Dan Cracchiolo**
Rob Polgar
Assistant to Mr Reeves
Reinaldo Puentes-Tucki
Assistant to Mr Fishburne
Sandra Hodge
2nd Unit Director
Bruce Hunt
1st Assistant Directors
Colin Fletcher
James McTeigue
2nd Unit:
Toby Pease
2nd Assistant Directors
Noni Roy
Tom Read
2nd Unit:
Jeremy Sedley
3rd Assistant Director
Paul Sullivan
Script Supervisors
Victoria Sullivan
2nd Unit:
Gillian Steine
Casting by
Mali Finn
Shauna Wolifson
Australian Casting
Mullinars Casting

Extras Casting
Tim Littleton
2nd Unit Director of
Photography
Ross Emery
Timelapse Cinematography
Simon Carroll Archive
Camera Operator
David Williamson
Camera/Steadicam
Operator
Robert Agganis
Underwater Camera
Operator
Roger Buckingham
Wescam Operator
Phil Pastahov
Cam-Remote Operator
Paul Micallef
1st Assistant Camera
David Elmes
2nd Unit:
Frank Flick
2nd Assistant Camera
Adrien Seffrin
Key Grips
Ray Brown
2nd Unit:
Toby Copping
Head Grip
Ian Bird
Dolly Grips
Mick Vivian
Mal Booth
Greg King
Aron Walker
2nd Unit:
Ben Hyde
Rigging Grip
David Hird
Gaffers
Reg Garside
2nd Unit:
Paul Johnstone
Best Boys
Alan Dunstan
2nd Unit:
Robbie Burr
Rigger Gaffers
Craig Bryant
Paul Cumming
Paul Moyes
Steve Johnston
Miles Jones
Chris Loveday

Ken Talbot
Colin Wyatt
Video Playback Operator
Michael Taylor
2nd Unit Video Operator
Anthony Toy
Stills Photographer
Jason Boland
Visual Effects Supervisor
John Gaeta
Visual Effects Producer
Matt Ferro
Visual Effects Editor
Kate Crossley
Assistant Visual Effects
Editors
Mary E. Walter
Allen Cappuccilli
Elizabeth Mercado
Manex Visual Effects, LLC
Associate VFX Supervisor:
Janek Sirrs
VFX Producer:
Alisoun F. Lamb
Digital FX Producer:
Diana Giorgiutti
Digital FX Supervisor:
Rodney Iwashina
Technology Supervisor:
Kim Libreri
Digital Line Producer:
Jeremy Beadell
Line Producer:
Paul Taglianetti
Production Aide:
Maureen Blume
Assistant Digital
Co-ordinator:
Noah Mizrahi
Production Aide (Australia):
Holly Radcliffe
Science Officer:
Dan Piponi
Software Development:
Jeremy Yarbrow
Lead Colour & Lighting TD:
Rudy Poat
Lead Shader Writer:
Steve Demers
Lead Technical Supervisor:
Ivo Kos
Compositor/Painter:
Amanda Evans
CG Designer/Animator:
Grant Niesner

FX Animator:
Al Arthur
Pre-viz Animator (Australia):
Nico Grey
3-D Texture Painter:
Brent Hartshorn
Texture Painter:
Devorah Petty
2-D Paint/Roto:
Jeff Allen
2-D/3-D Paint:
Jay Johnson
Conceptual Art:
Steve Burg
Matte Painting:
Charles Darby
Systems Manager:
Martin Weaver
Systems Admin:
Charles Henrich
Systems Support:
Victor E. Vaile IV
Deborah Thomas
Mark Burns
Editors:
Roy Berkowitz
Anthony Mark
Brian Porter
Film Recorder:
Greg Shimp
Character Animators:
Matt Farell
Jamie Pilgrim
John Lee
Andrew Schneider
Michael Ffish Hemschoot
Animators/Modellers:
Daniel Klem
Sean White
Enrique Vila
Technical Supervisors:
John Volny
Joseph Littlejoh
Lewis Siegel
Jason Wardle
Gil Baron
Michael McNeill
Sophia S. Longoria
John A. Tissavary
Compositors:
Barney Robson
John P. Nugent
Mary Leitz
Laura Hanigan
Daniel P. Rosen

Bullet Time
R&D/Technical Supervisor:
George Borshukov
Character Animator:
Gerard Benjamin Pierre
Technical Consultant:
Mark Weingartner
Pre-viz Animator:
Rob Nunn
R&D:
Bill Collis
2-D Animator:
Art David
Animator:
Daniel Sunwoo
Compositors:
John F. Sasaki
J. D. Cowles
Thomas Proctor
Technicians:
Paul Clemente
Frank Gallego
David Nunez
Sokkia Survey Crew:
Kirk Bolte
Andrew Borscz
DFilm Services
Executive Producer:
Peter Doyle
Digital Effects Supervisor:
Jon Thum
Digital FX Producer:
Alaric McAusland
Computer Animation
Supervisor:
Sally Goldberg
Animation Supervisor:
Ian McGuffie
Editorial Supervisor:
Jane MacGuire
Editor Assistant:
Natacha Tedeschi
Technology Manager:
Paul Ryan
Production Co-ordinator:
Rebecca Fox
Digital Composite
Supervisors:
Tim Crosbie
Mark Nettleton
Digital Compositors:
Stephen Lunn
David Hodson
Rotoscope Artists:
Elizabeth Carlon

Vanessa White
CGI Lead Animators:
Dominic Parker
Daniele Colajacomo
CGI Animators:
Justin Martin
Rangi Sutton
Animal Logic Film
VFX Supervisor:
Lynne Cartwright
CGI Artist/Colourist:
David Dulac
Programmer:
Justen Marshall
CGI Designer:
Jane Milledge
System Admin:
Ron Korpi
CGI Artists:
Lindsay Fleay
Andrew Quinn
Ben Gunsberger
Inferno Artists:
Kirsty Millar
John Breslin
Robin Cave
Krista Jordan
Compositors:
Charlie Armstrong
Grant Everett
Maryanne Lauric
Production Aide:
Edweana Wenkart
Producer:
Zareh Nalbandian
I/O Supervisor:
Naomi Hatchman
Screen Graphics:
Thomas Kayser
Additional Visual Effects
Amalgamated Pixels
Special Effects Supervisors
Steve Courtley
Brian Cox
Special Effects
Co-ordinator
Robina Osbourne
Special Effects
Rodney Burke
Monty Feiguth
David Pride
Arthur Spink Jr
Dave Young
Arran Gordon
Richard Alexander

Brian Belcher
Nick Beryk
Jeffrey Briggs
Darren De Costa
Paul Fenn
Lloyd Finnemore
Ray Fowler
Bernard Golenko
David Goldie
Paul Gorrie
Pauline Grebert
Leo Henry
David James
Jim Leng
Judy Mae Lewis
Shane Murphy
John Neal
Brigid Oulsnam
Peter Owens
Daniel Patmore
Garry Philips
Pieter Plooy
Reece Robinson
Lou Stefanel
Edwin Treasure
Thomas Van Koeverden
Walter Van Veenandaal
Kerry Williams
Sophie Dick
2nd Unit:
Kimble Hilder
Patrick Carmiggelt
Miniatures & Models
Supervisor
Tom Davies
Graphics
Karen Harborow
Screen Graphics
Co-ordinator
Adam McCulloch
Screen Graphics Assistant
Sami MacKenzie-Kerr
1st Assistant Editors
Peter Skarratt
USA:
Catherine Chase
Australia:
Noelleen Westcombe
Assistant Editors
Tom Costain
Jennifer Hicks
John Lee
Basia Ozerski
Conceptual Designer
Geofrey Darrow

2-D/3-D Conceptual Designer
Sergei Chadiloff
Art Directors
Hugh Bateup
Michelle McGahey
Assistant Art Directors
Jules Cook
Fiona Scott
Tony Williams
Art Department Co-ordinator
Trish Foreman
Art Department Researcher
Tara Kamath
Set Designers
Sarah Light
Jacinta Leong
Godric Cole
Judith Harvey
Andrew Powell
Deborah Riley
Set Decorators
Tim Ferrier
Lisa 'Blitz' Brennan
Marta McElroy
Illustrator
Phil Shearer
Scenic Artist
Peter Collias
Storyboard Artists
Steve Skroce
Tani Kunitake
Collin Grant
Warren Manser
Property Master
Lon Lucini
Props
Murray Gosson
Adrienne Ogle
Katie Sharrock
2nd Unit:
James Cox
Jake Clifton
Shane Bennett
Construction Supervisor
Phil Worth
Construction Co-ordinator
Marianne Evans
Construction
John Pickering
Andrew Staig
Marcus Smith
Tony Bardolph
Brett Bartlett

Mark Gatt
Terence Lord
Wayne Porter
John Rega
Trevor Smith
Standby Painters
Tony Piliotis
Jon Stiles
Costume Designer
Kym Barrett
Costume Supervisor
Lyn Askew
Costumers
Mary Lou Da Roza
Andrea Hood
Andrew Infanti
Pauline Walker
Jenny Irwin
Helen Mather
Nick Godlee
Fiona Holly
Nicole Brown
2nd Unit Wardrobe
Fiona Nicholls
Hero Eye wear Designed by
Richard Walker of Blind Optics
Footwear Designed by
Airwalk
Key Make-up Artist
Nikki Gooley
2nd Unit Make-up Artist
Kathy Courtney
Mr Fishburne's Make-up
Deborah Taylor
Assistant Make-up
Sherry Hubbard
Make-up Special Effects Designed and Created by
Bob McCarron
Senior Make-up SPFX Artist
Wendy Sainsbury
Make-up SPFX Artists
Rick Connelly
Sonja Smuk
Elka Wardega
Animatronic Prosthetics Created by
Makeup Effects Group Studio
Paul Katte
Nick Nicolaou
Animatronics Designer
Trevor Tighe
AMX Programmer
John Turner

Hairdresser
Cheryl Williams
Assistant Hairdresser
Simon Zanker
Titles Designed by
Greenberg/Schluter
Titles and Opticals by
Pacific Title/Mirage
Colour Timer
David Orr
Music Editors
Lori Eschler Frystak
Zigmund Gron
Music Score Recorded by
Armin Steiner
Music Score Mixed by
Larry Mah
Soundtrack Album on
Maverick Records
Soundtrack
'Dissolved Girl' by Robert Del Naja, Grantley Marshall, Andrew Vowles, Sara J. and Matt Schwartz, performed by Massive Attack (Courtesy of Virgin Records Ltd. By Arrangement with Virgin Records America, Inc.); 'Dragula (Hot Rod Herman Mix)' by Rob Zombie, Scott Humphrey, performed by Rob Zombie (Courtesy of Geffen Records. Under licence from Universal Music Special Markets); 'Mindfields' by Liam Howlett, performed by Prodigy (Courtesy of Maverick Recording Company/XL Recordings/Beggar's Banquet. By Arrangement with Warner Special Products); 'Leave You Far Behind (Lunatics Roller Coaster Mix)' by Simon Shackleton, Howard Saunders, performed by Lunatic Calm (Courtesy of Universal Music [UK] Ltd. Under licence from Universal Music Special Markets); 'Clubbed to Death (Kurayamino Mix)' by Rob Dougan, performed by Rob D (Courtesy of A&M Records Limited/Universal-Island Records. Under licence from

Universal Music Special Markets); 'Prime Audio Soup' by Jack Dangers, C. Dodd, performed by Meat Beat Manifesto (Courtesy of Nothing Records & Play It Again Sam/Heartbeat Records. Under licence from Universal Music Special Markets); 'Begin the Run' from *Night of the Lepus* by Jimmie Haskell; 'Minor Swing' by Django Reinhardt, Stephane Grappelli, performed by Django Reinhardt (Courtesy of The RCA Records Label of BMG Entertainment); 'I'm Beginning to See the Light' by Duke Ellington, Don George, Johnny Hodges, Harry James, performed by Duke Ellington (Courtesy of The RCA Records Label of BMG Entertainment); 'Spybreak!' by Alex Gifford, performed by Propellerheads (Courtesy of DreamWorks Records/Wall of Sound. Under licence from Universal Music Special Markets/ Propellerheads); 'Wake Up' by Zack De La Rocha, Brad Wilk, Tim Commerford, Tom Morello, performed by Rage against the Machine (Courtesy of Epic Records. By Arrangement with Sony Music Licensing); 'Rock Is Dead' by Marilyn Manson, Twiggy Ramirez, Madonna Wayne Gacy, performed by Marilyn Mason (Courtesy of Nothing/Interscope Records. Under licence from Universal Music Special Markets)

Sound Designer/ Supervising Sound Editor
Dane A. Davis
Sound Recordist
David Lee
Boom Operators
Jack Friedman
Gerry Nucifora
Re-recording Mixers
John Reitz,
Gregg Rudloff
David Campbell

2nd Stage
Kevin Carpenter
1st Assistant Sound Editor
Nancy Barker
Assistant Sound Editors
Barbara Delpuech
David McRell
Frank Long
Dialogue Editors
Charles Ritter
Susan Dudeck
Sound Effects Editors
Julia Evershade
Eric Lindemann
David Grimaldi
ADR Mixer
Tom O'Connell
Foley Artists
John Roesc
Hilda Hodges
Foley Mixers
Mary Jo Lang
Carolyn Tapp
Supervising Foley Editor
Thom Brennan
Foley Editor
Valerie Davidson
Negative Cutter
Mo Henry
Kung Fu Choreographer
Yuen Wo Ping
Hong Kong Kung Fu Co-ordinator
Carol Kim
Hong Kong Kung Fu Team
Yuen Eagle Shun Yi
Huang Sam Kai Sen
Lam Dion Tat Ho
Lee Chew Tat Chiu
Chen Tiger Hu
Leung Madye Sing Hung
Nils Bendix
Daxing Zhang
Stunt Co-ordinator
Glenn Boswell
Assistant Stunt Co-ordinator
Phil Meacham
Stunts
Ray Anthony
Greg Blandy
Richard Boue
Scott Brewer
Dave Brown

Todd Bryant
Michael Corrigan
Harry Dakanali
Dar Davies
Terry Flanagan
Scotty Gregory
Johnny Hallyday
Brian Ellison
Lou Horvath
Nigel King
Alex Kiss
Alex Kuzelicki
Ian Lind
Scott McLean
Phil Meacham
Chris Mitchell
Tony Lynch
Darren Mitchell
Steve Morris
Brett Praed
Brit Sooby
Sotiri Sotiropoulos
Glenn Sutor
Bernadette Van Gyen
Marijke Van Gyen
Mick Van Moorsel
Warwick Young
Stunt Doubles
Neo:
Chad Stahelski
Darko Tuskan
Neo/Agent Smith:
Paul Doyle
Trinity:
Annette Van Moorsel
Morpheus:
Andre Chyna McCoy
Agent Brown:
Shea Adams
Agent Jones:
Nigel Harbach
Switch:
Gillian Statham
Cypher:
Bob Bowles
Mouse:
Nash Edgerton
Dialogue Coach
Suzanne Celeste
Key Armourer
John Bowring
Action Vehicle Co-ordinators
John Allan
Tapio Piitulainen

Physical Trainers
Denise Snyder
Michelle Rowe
Cast Sports Masseuse
'Longy' Nguyin
Medical Advisers
Dr Ian I. T. Armstrong, M.D.
Dr Joseph M. Horrigan, D.C.
Publicist
Fiona Searson
Safety Co-ordinator
Lawrence Woodward
Safety Officers
Spike Cherrie
Kerry Blakeman
2nd Unit:
Brian Ellison
Nurses
Jacquie Robertson
2nd Unit:
Helen Cox
Caterers
Kevin Varnes
Kerry Fetzer
Guy Firth
2nd Unit:
John Faithful
Julie-Anne Lincoln
Aerial Co-ordinator
Terry Lee
Picture Helicopter Pilot
Greg Duncombe
Camera Helicopter Pilot
Gary Ticehurst
The Prisoner Clip Provided by
PolyGram Filmed
Entertainment
The Producers Wish to Thank the Following
The City of Sydney Council;
The NSW Premier's
Department; The NSW Film &
Television Office; CASA; The
Maritime Centre, Sydney;
Streetlights Program; AMX

Cast
Keanu Reeves
Thomas Anderson, 'Neo'
Laurence Fishburne
Morpheus
Carrie-Anne Moss
Trinity
Hugo Weaving
Agent Smith
Gloria Foster
Oracle
Joe Pantoliano
Cypher
Marcus Chong
Tank
Paul Goddard
Agent Brown
Robert Taylor
Agent Jones
Julian Arahanga
Apoc
Matt Doran
Mouse
Belinda McClory
Switch
Anthony Ray Parker
Dozer
David Aston
Rhineheart
Marc Gray
Choi
Ada Nicodemou
Dujour
Deni Gordon
priestess
Rowan Witt
spoon boy
Elenor Witt
Tamara Brown
Janaya Pender
Adryn White
Natalie Tjen
potentials
Bill Young
lieutenant
David O'Connor
FedEx man

Jeremy Ball
businessman
Fiona Johnson
woman in red
Harry Lawrence
old man
Steve Dodd
blind man
Luke Quinton
security guard
Lawrence Woodward
guard
Michael Butcher
cop who captures Neo
Bernie Ledger
big cop
Robert Simper
Chris Scott
cops
Nigel Harbach
parking cop
Martin Grelis
helicopter pilot

12,240 feet
136 minutes 10 seconds
(15 feet 7 frames cut in UK)

Dolby Digital/DTS/SDDS
Colour by
Atlab Australia
Prints by
Technicolor
2.35:1 [Super 35]

MPAA: 36569

Filmed on location in Sydney,
Australia, and at Fox Studios,
Australia

Credits compiled by
Markku Salmi

The Matrix is available on DVD
from Warner Home Video.

Bibliography

This book benefited from discussions with the scholars Carol Clover, Greil Marcus, Christopher Nealon, and Louis-Georges Schwartz, in addition to personal interviews with some members of The Matrix cast and crew (quotations appear herein from Keanu Reeves and Laurence Fishburne).

Althusser, Louis, 'Ideology and the Ideological State Apparatus', Lenin and Philosophy (Monthly Review), pp. 127–186.

Baudrillard, Jean, Simulations, trans. by Paul Foss et al. (New York: Semiotext(e), 1983).

————, Simulacra & Simulation, trans. by Sheila Faria Grazier (Ann Arbor: University of Michigan Press, 1994).

Borges, Jorge Luis, Collected Fictions, trans. by Andrew Hurley (New York: Viking, 1998).

'Bowling-Alley Owner Wants TV Ad To Look "More Matrix-y"', The Onion, vol. 39 no. 25.

Bukatman, Scott, Blade Runner (London: BFI Modern Classics, 1997).

Clark, T. J., The Painting of Modern Life (Princeton, NJ: Princeton University Press, 1999).

Dancy, Jonathan, An Introduction to Contemporary Epistemology (London: Blackwell, 1986).

Dark, Jane, 'Reloaded Questions', Village Voice, New York, May 14-20, 2003.

Dick, Philip K., Do Androids Dream of Electric Sheep?, (New York: Del Rey, 1996).

Freud, Sigmund, The Schreber Case, trans. by Andrew Webber (London and New York: Penguin, 2003).

Gibson, William, Neuromancer (New York: Ace, 1995).

————, Burning Chrome (New York: Eos, 2003).

Haber, Karen (ed.), Exploring the Matrix: Visions of the Cyber Present (New York: St Martin's Press, 2003).

Irwin, William (ed.), The Matrix and Philosophy: Welcome to the Desert of the Real (Popular Culture and Philosophy, vol. 3; Chicago: Open Court 2002).

Lamm, Spencer, 'Crew Interview: Bill Pope', whatisthematrix.warnerbros.com.

Lane, Anthony, 'City of God', New Yorker, 20 January 2003.

Liu, Alan, The Laws of Cool: Knowledge Work and the Culture of Information. (Chicago, IL: University of Chicago Press, 2004).

Marin, Louis, Utopiques, jeux d'espaces (Paris: Éditions de Minuit, 1973).

Marx, Karl, The German Ideology: Including Thesis on Feuerbach (Amherst, NY: Prometheus, 1998).

————, Capital: A Critique of Political Economy, trans. by Ben Fowkes (London and New York: Penguin, 1992).

McLuhan, Marhsall and Lapaham, Lewis H., Understanding Media: The Extensions of Man (Cambridge: MIT Press, 1994).

Schwartz, Louis-Georges, 'Bad Affect: Misery in Service of The Revolution', conference paper presented October 2002, Society for Psychoanalysis and Social Change, University of Pennsylvania.

Sterling, Bruce (ed.), Mirrorshades: The Cyberpunk Anthology (New York: Ace, 1988).

Stevens, Wallace, The Palm at the End of the Mind (New York: Vintage, 1990).

U.S. Government, 2002 Compendium of Major Financial Reports to the SEC by Twelve Companies under Scrutiny or In the News: Adelphia Communications, AOL Time Warner, Enron, Global Crossing, Halliburton, ImClone Systems, Martha Stewart Living Omnimedia, Merrill Lynch, Polaroid, Qwest, WorldCom, and Xerox (Washington: Progressive Management, 2002).

'Videogame Industry Booming', Game Market Watch, gamemarketwatch.com, 3 May 2002.

Williams, Raymond. Keywords (New York: Oxford University Press, 1983).

Yeffeth, Glenn, and David Gerrold (eds), Taking the Red Pill: Science, Philosophy and Religion in The Matrix (Dallas. TX: BenBella, 2003)

Žižek, Slavoj, 'The Matrix, or, The Two Sides of Perversion', paper presented at 'Inside the Matrix' international symposium, Center for Art and Media, Karlsruhe, 1999.

————, Enjoy Your Symptom!: Jacques Lacan in Hollywood and Out (New York: Routledge, 2001).

————, Welcome to the Desert of the Real (London: Verso, 2002).

Also Published

Amores Perros
Paul Julian Smith (2003)

L'Argent
Kent Jones (1999)

Blade Runner
Scott Bukatman (1997)

Blue Velvet
Michael Atkinson (1997)

Caravaggio
Leo Bersani & Ulysse Dutoit
(1999)

A City of Sadness
Bérénice Reynaud (2002)

Crash
Iain Sinclair (1999)

The Crying Game
Jane Giles (1997)

Dead Man
Jonathan Rosenbaum
(2000)

**Dilwale Dulhaniya Le
Jayenge**
Anupama Chopra (2002)

Don't Look Now
Mark Sanderson (1996)

Do the Right Thing
Ed Guerrero (2001)

Easy Rider
Lee Hill (1996)

The Exorcist
Mark Kermode (1997,
2nd edn 1998,
rev. 2nd edn 2003)

Eyes Wide Shut
Michel Chion (2002)

Groundhog Day
Ryan Gilbey (2004)

Heat
Nick James (2002)

The Idiots
John Rockwell (2003)

Independence Day
Michael Rogin (1998)

Jaws
Antonia Quirke (2002)

L.A. Confidential
Manohla Dargis (2003)

Last Tango in Paris
David Thompson (1998)

**Nosferatu – Phantom der
Nacht**
S. S. Prawer (2004)

**Once Upon a Time in
America**
Adrian Martin (1998)

Pulp Fiction
Dana Polan (2000)

The Right Stuff
Tom Charity (1997)

**Saló or The 120 Days of
Sodom**
Gary Indiana (2000)

Seven
Richard Dyer (1999)

**The Shawshank
Redemption**
Mark Kermode (2003)

The Silence of the Lambs
Yvonne Tasker (2002)

The Terminator
Sean French (1996)

Thelma & Louise
Marita Sturken (2000)

The Thing
Anne Billson (1997)

**The 'Three Colours'
Trilogy**
Geoff Andrew (1998)

Titanic
David M. Lubin (1999)

Trainspotting
Murray Smith (2002)

Unforgiven
Edward Buscombe (2004)

The Usual Suspects
Ernest Larsen (2002)

The Wings of the Dove
Robin Wood (1999)

Withnail & I
Kevin Jackson (2004)

**Women on the Verge of a
Nervous Breakdown**
Peter William Evans (1996)

**WR – Mysteries of the
Organism**
Raymond Durgnat (1999)

BFI MODERN CLASSICS

BFI Modern Classics combine careful research with high-quality writing about contemporary cinema.

If you would like to receive further information about future **BFI Modern Classics** or about other books from BFI Publishing, please fill in your name and address and return this card to us.*
(No stamp required if posted in the UK, Channel Islands, or Isle of Man.)

NAME

ADDRESS

POSTCODE

WHICH **BFI MODERN CLASSIC** DID YOU BUY?

* In USA and Canada, please return your card to:
University of California Press, 2120 Berkeley Way,
Berkeley, CA 94720 USA

BFI Publishing
21 Stephen Street
FREEPOST 7
LONDON
W1E 4AN